Vander Zalm's
Northwest Gardener's Almanac

Bill Vander Zalm

hancock

house

ISBN 0-88839-163-3

Copyright © 1982 Bill Vander Zalm

Cataloging in Publication Data

Vander Zalm, Bill
Vander Zalm's Northwest gardener's almanac

1. Gardening — Northwest, Pacific. I. Title.
II. Title: Northwest gardener's almanac
SB453.3.C2V36   635   C82-091260-3

Development Editor and Graphic Consultant Peggy Reine Cromer
Editors Kelly Allen & Susan Gillis
Typeset by Lisa Smedman & Verlee Webb in Times Roman on an AM Varityper Comp/Edit
Production, Layout & Cover Design Crystal Ryan
Illustrations by Chris Kielesinski
Printed in Canada by Friesen Printers

Hancock House Publishers Ltd.
19313 Zero Avenue, Surrey, B.C., Canada V3S 5J9
Hancock House Publishers
1431 Harrison Avenue, Blaine, WA 98230

Contents

May

Foreword

However engaged I might be in public affairs, I can never cut myself off from the interest and genuine love I have for growing things. To dig the earth, plant, and nurture growing things is as natural to me as breathing.

There are many books on gardening. I dare say there are probably more books on growing things than on any other topic. No one book can tell you everything. I think the books that feature specific things—pruning, vegetables, roses, and so on—are very helpful and certainly worth the investment. Serious gardeners should always have a small library of reference.

So, having said that no one book can tell you everything, I'm admitting this book can't either. However, in the years I've been in the nursery business, I've found that dedicated gardeners like to take hints from more than one source. The question box that appeared in my weekly columns proved this: although many readers had already found solutions to their gardening problems, they still wanted confirmation from me. A most flattering thing to happen, but again, I repeat, take bits and pieces from all the experts and select those which seem to work best for you. If this book is used as a handy reference, it can guide you through many month-by-month chores that will make your gardening most rewarding. Often it's the little things you do, both simple and economical, that spell success with your gardening endeavors.

We'll talk a little about pruning, vegetable gardens, bedding plants, hydroponic growing, companion planting, and generally go into a potpourri of hints, do's and don'ts, and even some "old wives' tales" that aren't so strange after all.

To those of you who share my enthusiasm for gardening, I hope this month-by-month guide will be helpful.

Happy shoveling!

Bill Vander Zalm

"The good Lord doesn't mind you praying for a good crop, but He expects you to get out the shovel and dig the field."

To my wife, Lillian, and my entire family, who support my belief that an investment in the soil is an investment yielding satisfaction beyond all else.

GLADIOLUS

GERANIUM

LUPINE

IRIS

THIS SIDE UP

C. Kiciesnoski

January

Start the new year off right

A whole new gardening year lies ahead, and no doubt many new products, techniques, and finds about the plant world will help make people's lives a little easier and happier.

What's to do in January? Quite a bit. I'll just briefly review what I do between Christmas and mid-January and let you catch up on what you might not have done; then we'll proceed with the month-by-month steps you need to take to have success. Just remember, timing is everything. There's a time to accomplish each chore and thereby cut down your overall workload.

Between Christmas and mid-January

When we have a particularly mild winter, and we usually do, around Christmas-time I get out the bamboo rake and move about the clumps of grass left on the lawn after the last cutting. There are usually a few dead patches here and there where the clumps are more concentrated, and with a good hard raking, the patches will fill in come early spring.

As I always mark where I've planted perennial plants, I can safely begin to spade over the beds and let air penetrate the soil for the next several months before actual planting.

I cover the soil with a generous application of white lime, 50 pounds per 2000 square feet (23 kilograms per 187 square meters), after spading, and leave it on top to wash in, sweeten the soil, and help break up the humus created by spading under the flower remains from last summer. I do the same for the vegetable garden, but keep the lime away from where I plant potatoes.

A mild winter also finds a few daffodils and crocuses pushing spring. I watch very carefully, for a cold snap could destroy these anxious plants. It's wise to have a few bags of sawdust (depending on the extent of the area where the spikes are protruding) on hand to sprinkle over the spikes to protect them from freezing, should

12

the weather suddenly change.

Flowering trees only need to have the water shoots and a few cross branches removed, plus a bit of shaping done.

The fruit trees, however, need considerably more. There are many pamphlets and books on pruning available at nurseries, but basically, the tree should be pruned to be strong—no weak shoots, water sprouts, weak crotches, or cross branches. The tree must also be pruned to allow plenty of sunlight into its center and to let breezes blow through freely, thus preventing the onset of disease.

Spraying is especially important. Generally, I use lime sulphur and dormant oil, but copper sulphate is another choice. Recommended mixes are always indicated on the container.

The main reason for lack of spraying success is the application. You can not effectively apply the spray mix with a hose attachment or a fly sprayer. You need the type of sprayer, manual or mechanical, that can put the spray on with sufficient pressure to penetrate every crack and crevice and make it stick.

Get all garden tools in top shape

Check tools for caked soil or rust. Soak any rusted tools overnight in a bucket of rust remover.

Check all tool handles for cracks and breaks. Sand down handles to avoid getting splinters. Wrap superficial cracks with waterproof tape. Replace handles that are severely damaged. Tools that break during use can often cause injuries.

Consider spray painting dull handles. Colorful handles prevent you from accidently stepping on or tripping over a tool left lying on the ground.

Sharpen tools or have them sharpened. Dull tools are more apt to slip, causing injury. Beware of oversharpening, as this presents a measure of danger also.

Check garden hoses for splits and holes. Cut out the damaged sections, and use metal couplings to rejoin the hose ends.

Check the lawnmower. Be sure blades are sharp. If electric, check the cord for cuts and exposed wiring. For power mowers, make sure you follow the manufacturer's instructions regarding clean oil, clean spark plugs, etc.

There is an old axiom that a poor workman blames his tools. In the case of gardening, you can be the best workman in your neighborhood, but poor tools will cause needless effort and not really do the job correctly.

Winter takes its toll on soil

The word "ecology" is beginning to take on a deeper meaning every day—maintaining the balance of nature and restoring to the earth that which is taken from it.

As we continue to grow crops in the field, in our own little vegetable garden, or in a flower plot, we often see a breakdown of the amount of soil fiber (the body of the soil) and, with winter rain, heavy cropping acidity tends to build up, but more noticeable is the diminishing availability of the major plant nutrients and minor elements. If the nitrogen, phosphate, and potash; the elements like iron, magnesium, boron, and zinc; the lime and fiber are not replaced, we end up with dead soil. The minute a vegetable stops growing it is in big trouble. We can add lime, manure, and fertilizer, but again, it is difficult to keep a proper balance, particularly with chemical fertilizers, and the elements are even more difficult to replace.

Growing the same crop in the same area year after year presents another set of problems. Some vegetables are light feeders, such as the root crops like beets, carrots, and onions; others are heavy feeders, such as the cabbage family, the leafy plants, the cucumbers, and tomatoes; while still others are soil restorers, like beans and peas. By moving these various kinds of vegetables around or interplanting, we add vigor to the soil as we go along. The other problem is that certain plants attract insects or are susceptible to a particular disease, while still others repel insects

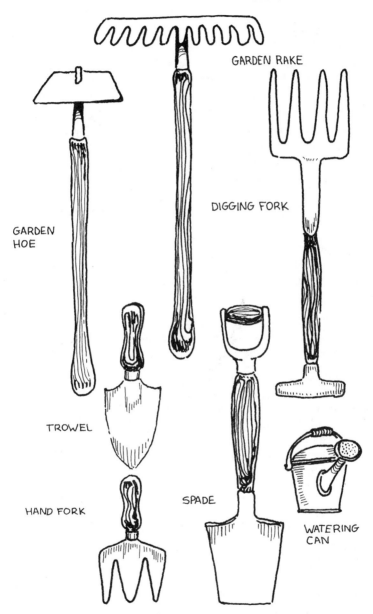

GARDEN TOOLS

GARDEN RAKE

GARDEN
HOE

DIGGING FORK

TROWEL

HAND FORK

SPADE

WATERING
CAN

and deter disease. For example, the marigold is very effective in soil infestations of the pesky nematode. Bear with me on my repetition of this gem. It bears repeating because it's so effective.

Some plants give off substances through their leaves and roots that affect other plants. Over the years, the aromas and exudates of plants have been observed and used to encourage better plant growth relationships as well as to repel insects.

Some of these compatibilities have been proven to be physical or chemical reactions. Still other plants provide nutrients to the soil, which they extract from the air, and these nutrients in turn feed other plants; for instance, pigweed loves the potato and the potato adores the pigweed. Nature often helps these plants get together, and if a certain weed is often seen growing with another plant, it is probably not by accident but because of mutual love.

I especially look forward to experimenting more with the various garden herbs, but generally we are learning a lot about nature and its ability to provide for itself. There is much more to learn.

Most of us know that farmers grow clover, beans, peas, or other such legumes for nitrogen fixing. This approach improves the fertility of the land and has been used for years.

In recent years, the importance of nitrogen fixing has become much more prominent. Plants that can make their own fertilizer are in greater demand in this era of energy shortages. Their ecological benefits have become recognized. Even molecular biologists have gotten into the act, talking about getting corn or wheat plants to fix their own nitrogen via gene transplants and genetic recombinations.

Imagine the potential for increased production when the plants that produce our food can also produce their own nutrients for greater growth!

It wasn't until more recently that plant biologists discovered that nature is even more wonderful than we knew it to be.

Did you ever wonder why those so-called pesky alder trees sprout up, creating what would seem like a nuisance among our valuable fir tree stands? Did you ever wonder why those trees

16

seem to crowd out the much more productive plants? Well, now we know.

Those alder trees are put there by nature for a purpose. It's now been shown that alder trees fix nitrogen the way legumes do, so a stand of alder can prepare a fertile soil to help grow the trees that build our houses. Nature is beautiful and provides far more effectively than man ever will. Man can either destroy or help nature and, fortunately, we are learning.

Companion planting is becoming more and more popular as we learn how plants can complement each other. Check your nurseries or bookstores for information on this topic.

Pronunciation is difficult, but names useful

Few can really pronounce them. It's tough, even for the best of us. But practice does help, and if you're in the business you must know a good number of them.

I'm often asked, "why those Latin names?" Then again, there's the lady who asks for a "heavenly plant" or a plant called "mother's favorite" or more commonly still, "blue bell plant," and I have to ask her, "Do you know the Latin name?"

Taraxacum officinale is a weed, though it is seldom called that. Most often we call it dandelion. But when someone talks about the buttercup, unless he mentions the Latin name, you won't know which of the forty-odd buttercups he means. In other words, we just have no better system for pinning down exactly which plant we're talking about.

Latin was originally chosen because it is universal and non-changing. So instead of trying to beat the system, let's join it and find out a little more.

Most of our garden plants are directly related to, and are much like, wild plants. Often their names tell you the color, form, and where first found. Their first name is the genus, a large group of plants that look much alike in form or shape. Our native wild tiger lily (*Lilium columbianum*) flowers in summer above 4,000 feet (1219 meters), especially along the Hope-Princeton Highway

17

in British Columbia. It belongs to the genus *Lilium*.

Water lilies (*nymphaea*), sword lilies (iris), day lilies (*hemerocallis*) and many others are not true lilies; in structure they vary considerably.

The second name, or species name, defines the plant even more; all plants belonging to the same species are almost identical to each other in shape, color, and size.

In my example, *Lilium columbianum, columbianum* is the species name, which means from British Columbia. Since there is only one *Lilium columbianum*, everybody knows what you are talking about when you use this name.

When this lily is put in a domestic garden, after multiplying it is indeed better than the regular wild form. It is obviously *Lilium columbianum*, but is has a certain something—a different curve to the petal, or it's larger, or it has a more golden hue. For the purpose of this example, say the lily was striped red and so is really a variegated form. Your new find thus becomes *Lilium columbianum variegatum*.

Now let's assume that you've really become excited about your find and you want to go one step further and make a cross between your *Lilium columbianum variegatum* and some other lily like *Lilium pardalinum*, the panther lily from the coast of Oregon and California. The offspring arrives and you now have a mixture of the characteristics of the two parents. It can be called *Lilium columbianum variegatum X Lilium pardalinum*. For convenience, use *Lilium columbianum variegatum pardalinum*.

Three more terms often used in the trade are hybrid, clone, and strain.

A hybrid is not a wild species but a cross between two or more of such species.

Clones are best defined by the way they are multiplied. Anything that is multiplied by cuttings, tubers, bulbs, budding, or graft is a clone; in other words, anything that is an identical, a "chip off the old block," but is not raised from seeds. Potato varieties, dahlias, tulips, daffodils, fuchsias, and geraniums, even Bartlett pears and McIntosh apples are clones. All plants belonging to a clone are absolutely alike in every respect.

Strains are plants raised from seed obtained as a specific result of the crossing between two known parents. The plants of a strain are always somewhat variable in size, shape, color, or other characteristics. Lilies are often sold as strains. They are cheaper than clones since they are raised from seed and they also present exciting surprises because of the slight variations.

Now is the time to start planning your vegetables

This is a great time to begin considering your plans for the vegetable garden.

Much of the work faced in spring garden preparation and continued summer maintenance can be reduced enormously through early planning of what should be done when, how, and where; which vegetables will be planted; and how the soil is best prepared. Companion planting is worth considering to ensure better growth, reduce disease, and discourage bugs.

The best vegetables to grow are those eaten fresh. If space is limited, there is no point to growing vegetables that require storing, as they can be purchased just as well at the store. On the other hand, if you freeze or can your surplus, there's both economy and pride of accomplishment. I've yet to taste commercially produced jams and jellies that can equal the homemade varieties.

Fresh radishes, lettuce, cut spinach, vine-ripened tomatoes, peas you eat minutes after picking, corn sweeter than any canned variety—these can never be bought field-fresh in the supermarket, not even at the country roadside market.

Some points to remember in the planning process

The minute a vegetable stops growing, it is in trouble. Vegetables need good soil, plenty of water, food, and sun.

With warm-season vegetables, the object is fruit rather than leaves, roots, or stems. Warm-season vegetables

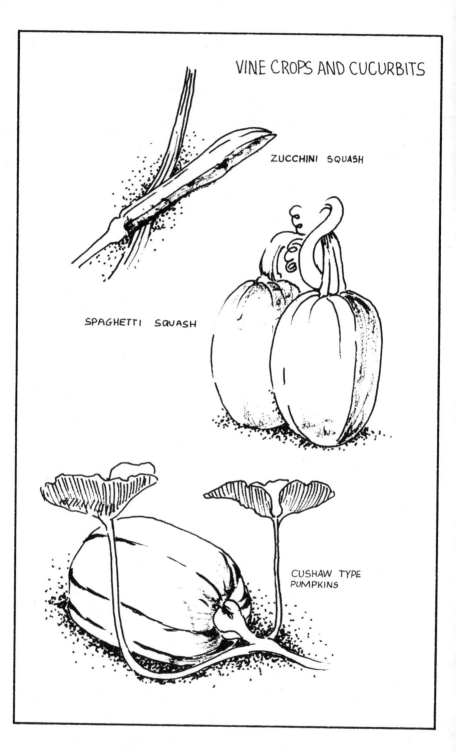

VINE CROPS AND CUCURBITS

ZUCCHINI SQUASH

SPAGHETTI SQUASH

CUSHAW TYPE
PUMPKINS

should not be planted too early. In our area the best time is after the first of May, and the spot in your vegetable plot should receive the greatest amount of heat and sun.

Cool-weather plants produce leaves of chard, spinach, lettuce, cabbage, or the immature flowers of cauliflower, broccoli, and root crops. These are only a few examples, but all should be planted in early spring or in late summer in order to have the most possible cool days. You can begin planting cabbage, lettuce, and others soon after the first of March.

Perennial vegetables are cool-weather items and thus will do better in cooler areas of the garden. The most common examples are rhubarb, asparagus, artichoke, and horseradish. These are best planted in fall or early spring. Root crops prefer a loose soil, and all but potatoes return the greatest pounds per square foot. Beets, carrots, onions, parsnips, radishes, and turnips all fall in this category.

Cole crops or cabbage family plants such as broccoli, Brussels sprouts, cabbage, cauliflower, collards, kale, and kohlrabi are cool-season plants and heavy feeders. They also like lime in the soil.

The legumes—snap beans, lima beans, and peas—are all available in bush and pole varieties and are basically cool-weather plants, though the snap beans like it warmer and the lima beans prefer it hot. Snap beans are among the best for the home garden.

Vine crops or cucurbit family plants include such members as the cucumbers, late melons, musk melons, pumpkins, squash, and watermelons. They are all warm-season growers. All of the cucurbits are heavy feeders. Most of them need a lot of space, although cucumbers can be grown on trellises or against a fence.

The solanaceous fruit group includes the familiar tomato, eggplant, and pepper. They are warm-weather plants. Tomatoes are a particular favorite of home gardeners everywhere. All you need is a few plants of any of these vegetables to give you an ample harvest. They are among the most popular vegetables sold by nurseries as young bedding plants.

Corn is a loner. It doesn't fit any of the other categories. Corn is a warm-season crop and very popular as a home garden vegetable.

There's plenty more to come, but this will give you a start in the planning process.

When planning, consider water requirements

Even though we are not unfamiliar with rain in many regions of the northwest, many areas fall under water restrictions. Just for fun, here are some water intake requirements for some of the things you may plan for your garden.

For every pound of lettuce you harvest from your garden, 300 pounds (135 kilograms) of water will be used in its growth.

If you drank as much as a corn plant, just to stay even with the water lost to the air each day, you would have to drink 10 to 14 gallons (30 to 50 liters) daily. That's between 160 and 240 glasses of water every day!

Lack of sufficient water causes radishes to become hard and woody, carrots stumpy, and lettuce bitter, and it causes tomatoes to drop blossoms.

When you don't water your plants with lukewarm water, it takes four to six hours for the soil to regain the heat loss to the cold water. The plant roots try to readjust instead of using their energy for their primary functions of growth.

Of course, you can't get lukewarm water out of a hose, so the last watering tip was meant for houseplants. However, if you water in the very early morning, your garden plants will do much better. Never water during the heat of the day, or when any of your plants are in direct sunlight. Ground watering, or irrigating,

WATERING METHODS

OVERHEAD
WATERING CAN

SURFACE
PUNCTURED HOSE

OVERHEAD
SPRINKLER

is always the preferable method for mature plants and vegetable crops.

Overhead watering suits most of the cool-season crops. Overhead watering will create a bit of the fog that goes with cool air. Overhead watering can damage hot-weather crops, especially squash and other vine crops, since it can cause mildew. It will also cause tomatoes to split.

Surface watering, done properly, will usually be most effective. It allows you to be more selective and provides a better opportunity to avoid under- or over-watering. There is also less chance of disease or burn of foliage.

Q: **I want to grow some herbs in my apartment. What can you recommend?**
A: Get a clay strawberry jardiniere and plant parsley, chives, mint, sage, rosemary (for fragrance), and thyme.

Q: **What is the herb that tastes to strong in Italian foods?**
A: Probably oregano, which is also great in scrambled eggs and on fish when caught and pan-fried right away.

February

Common sense will guide you to the right spot for your garden

If you keep the basic requirements of all vegetables in mind—sun, water, and fertile soil—common sense will guide you in choosing the right spot for them and preparing it for planting.

Because vegetables need full sun, the plot should be far enough from large trees or buildings to avoid shade. If one end of the garden gets more sun than the other, plant the fruiting crops at that end and the leaf and root crops where it may be shady part of the day.

Tree roots compete with vegetables for water and food. As a rule of thumb to help determine how far away from the tree you should plant, remember that a tree's roots spread out about as far as its branches. If you must put the leaf and root crops in a place where tree roots do compete with them, double up on the amount of fertilizer and water that you normally give those crops.

A level location is better than a hill or bank, since the water will go down into the soil instead of running off.

If your garden is on a slope, plant the vegetables as they do in Japan: on shelves that you can flood.

Because vegetables do grow very fast and are heavy eaters, feed in quantity. Manure is still my favorite for vegetables. Work it in at planting time, if it is well rotted.

The perfect soil for vegetables is a loose, fertile, well-drained loam. Neutral soil is best. Most vegetables fail or do poorly if the soil is too acid. Agricultural white lime applied during winter or early spring, before you spade, at the rate of 50 pounds per 1,500 to 2,000 square feet (25 kilograms per 140 to 200 square meters), is usually recommended.

Lime has more than sweetener. It improves the texture of both heavy and light soils, and helps to release such vital elements as phosphate and potash that might otherwise lie dormant.

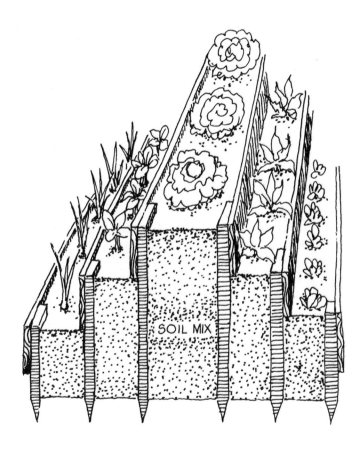

SOIL SHELVES TO HELP DRAINAGE ON
STEEPLY SLOPED LAND

The soil should be well watered before you plant, not after. Test the soil texture at the time of planting by taking a handful and squeezing it. If it balls up when you squeeze, it's too wet; if it crumbles, it's just right.

Weeds have no place among vegetables because they take nutrients and water away from the root area. Hoe them out at first sight. It is better to scrape than to chop; don't dig in deep or you'll ruin the hard-working feeder roots on your vegetable plants. Water and nutrients enter the roots through the growing root tips, often just beneath the surface.

Many northwest gardeners like to mulch their vegetable plants. Apply a sawdust mulch or peat moss as a blanket about 1 to 2 inches (2½ to 5 centimeters) thick. I prefer peat moss, though it's much more expensive. Peat moss will not rob the soil of nitrogen, while sawdust often does. The mulch will save much watering and weeding, and allow for a more even soil temperature, as well as cut down on slug damage. It will also prevent rotting fruits from coming into contact with the soil.

All vegetables are heavy feeders. If your soil is naturally rich in nutrients, you've partly got it made, though you'll find that sooner or later you'll need to add the occasional boost.

The quickest, easiest, and most effective way to correct soil food deficiencies is to add a commercial fertilizer. It contains the important nitrogen, phosphorus, and potash. For row crops, it is most convenient to apply the fertilizer in bands 2 to 3 inches (5 to 7 centimeters) from the plants and 2 to 3 inches (5 to 7 centimeters) deep. For the proper amount, follow the directions on the package. Cover the fertilizer with soil and water thoroughly. Best results will be obtained by using a small amount more often, rather than a whole lot all at once.

For root crops, the most popular fertilizer is one low on nitrogen and higher in phosphate and potash.

For leaf crops, the most popular fertilizer is one higher in nitrogen, and for fruiting crops, we need plenty of potash.

You might reread this section in May, after most of your planting is done, to consider mulching and to check fertilizer tips.

Some pointers on houseplants

Although I cover houseplant care quite extensively in the October section, I don't want to risk losing readers so early in the book. Obviously not everyone grows a vegetable garden, or, for that matter, even has a garden area, so here are a few general comments on houseplants.

From tropical forest to your front room is a difficult step for plants to adjust to. Because of this, there have been great efforts over the years to select and hybridize those types and varieties best able to adjust to growing in a pot.

The term "houseplants" applies to a large group of plants suitable for indoors over a long period of time. Most are tropical plants that do not go dormant or drop leaves, and many bloom, often for a long time.

In our climate, winter growth is limited unless, of course, sun lamps are used, in which case some growth will occur even in the darkest months of winter.

There are many varieties of tropical houseplants and many will require varying conditions. However, it is well to consider the area from which they originate in nature.

The tropicals from the deep south such as ficus, dieffenbachia, philodendron, and yucca, require conditions that differ from those which originate in the subtropics or the desert. The real tropicals can take a relatively steady temperature, while the subtropicals and desert succulents or cactuses prefer cool nights.

Very often I'm asked, "Why doesn't my cactus bloom?" Well, a cactus in the desert blooms during the no-growth period of winter when days are warm but nights are very cool. In our homes the night temperatures are often too warm, and thus the cactuses never really quit growing. I mentioned subtropical plants as also preferring cooler nighttime temperatures. Among this group are palms, ferns, bougainvillea, oleander, fuchsias, geraniums, fatsia, citrus, and passion flowers.

Leafy plants are most popular. The leaf colors and forms make attractive arrangements in large pots or planters. The flowering plants are also becoming more and more popular. There are few homes without an African violet; poinsettias and Christmas cactuses are commonplace everywhere in winter; primulas and cinerarias in spring; gloxinias in summer; and kalanchoes or star of Bethlehem in fall. The longest-lasting flowering plants include such favorites as hibiscus, flowering maple, azaleas, and cyclamen.

Not everyone will have success with the same plants. Much depends on the type of heat and light, but also some people have a feel for certain plants. Some of my friends can grow African violets with little effort and always have a show of bloom, while other can't get even one flower but grow rubber plants six feet tall.

A home without plants is dull. Plants provide much pleasure and are living partners in the home, just like people and pets. And like people and animals, plants need a little attention.

In their artificial surroundings, plants can not provide for themselves. It's up to you to make them feel at home by providing an atmosphere as close as possible to their natural environment.

A ficus grows in areas often subject to drought and thus likes to go somewhat dry between generous waterings. The umbrella plant grows along the river banks in the subtropics and therefore wants its feet wet all of the time. An African violet wants light but not direct sun, while a christthorn prefers to bake in it.

Plants have their hang-ups and dislikes. To name a few: drafts, people and animals walking past, temperature changes, constant turning or changing of positions, too high or too low a temperature, and constant overwatering. Hairy-leafed plants don't like to be sponged.

Plants can become diseased or bug infested, but this most often happens when your plant is unhappy because of handling or position.

A happy plant is able to withstand most onslaughts. Disease, though not common, is very difficult to treat in the living room. Because it can spread quickly, diseased plants are most often simply disposed of. Bugs are more common, with red spiders being the most common pest. They tend to attack dry plants, as they hate moisture; plants that are sprayed fairly regularly are not likely to be a harboring place.

Again, in the October chapter, you'll find information on proper feeding and watering practices, two of the most vital operations to insure steady, healthy growth.

If you have a clematis vine, this month you can cut back all the previous year's growth, virtually to ground level. See the March chapter for specific information on clematis care and pruning.

Q: **I'd like to try to master a houseplant different from those all my neighbors have. What's a good choice?**

A: I have just obtained the most beautiful specimen for Lillian and myself, and I'm sure you'll be pleased trying this one. It's the anthurium. The exotic flowers of the anthurium have a distinct air of luxury—large, waxy bracts, each with a colored tail at its center. The flowering period extends over many months, and each bloom lasts for many weeks. The easiest variety of anthurium to grow is the flamingo flower variety; the more difficult are the painter's palette and the crystal anthurium. Secrets of success with this plant are temperature, light, and air humidity. It requires average warmth; the minimum temperature in winter is 60°F (15°C). Protect it from summer sun, but keep in bright light in winter. Mist the leaves frequently to maintain a humid atmosphere. Give your anthurium a little water every few days to keep the soil moist, but never waterlogged. Use soft, tepid water.

March

Use great care with spring pruning of trees

In early March few people I talk to have pruned or sprayed their trees, let alone limed the lawn or garden. When the sun does break, every nursery garden center will work triple time to keep up.

There's one consolation: all the rain that falls now will not fall later. We'll again enjoy a beautiful spring and still better summer.

If there's one who says he's not far behind with the gardening, we'll put him to the truth test: "Bite a pure horseradish root and if you keep your eyes open, you've passed."

We can't do all things at once, so we'll do the most urgent first. For the first week, let's resolve to concentrate on the pruning.

The right tools make it easier

A pole pruner, lopper, pruning saw, pruning shear, and can of tree emulsion (tree paint) with a handy putty knife are all the tools we need. Promise yourself that every time the rain lets up, you'll prune at least one tree.

Pruning plants and trees is done to increase the capacity for flowering or fruiting, to improve their appearance, and to strengthen and make them live longer.

Pruning doesn't change a tree's natural habit but it can help direct growth. As the old saying goes, "As the twig is bent, so the tree will grow."

The first consideration in pruning is to decide the shape. Do you want the main leader or pyramid shape, the open center or base shape, the umbrella shape, or the modified leader shape?

The main leader shape is the one most often used for shade trees like oak, birch, ash, beech, and maple.

Once you have established the height you want, go to the first branch from the ground and work a framework of well-spaced branches around the trunk.

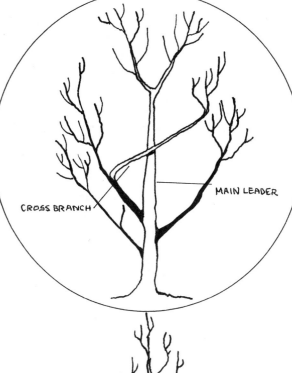

CROSS BRANCH

MAIN LEADER

CENTRAL LEADER

OPEN CENTER

MODIFIED LEADER

BASIC SHAPES

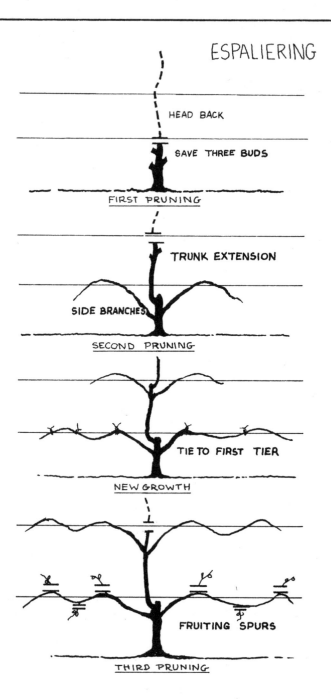

There's little pruning to be done in the following years except to remove a crossing or broken branch.

The open center or base shape is used for flowering prunes, plums, cherries, crabs, hawthorns, and trees that do not grow tall. You can begin when the tree is young by selecting four or five strong branches spaced around the trunk. Instead of cutting the lower ones way back, try to keep them all about the same height, but do take out the main leader.

In future years keep a main leader from establishing itself and keep the center free from cross branches; thin where crowding is obvious, remove those branches that go straight up, and just let the natural growth do the rest.

The umbrella-shaped tree is found mainly with weeping varieties like the weeping cherries, crabapples, mulberries, ash, and dwarf maples. These trees require little pruning except, for instance, the removal of cross branches.

The modified leader is used mainly for fruit trees where we prune for form and strength rather than appearance. Most damage to mature fruit trees occurs at a crotch.

Fruit trees, when properly pruned, will have three or four main branches at wide angles to the trunk. It is important to maintain the leader in the main role, but it should not be as prominent as the main leader (or pyramid) pruning of shade trees.

The tree must be kept relatively open to let the sunshine in and breezes blow through. This will permit better fruiting with less chance of disease.

Too heavy a pruning delays bearing, especially for older trees. "Little and often" should be the rule.

Peach trees require the most pruning, especially when young. A pruned peach tree should look like little more than a skeleton.

Pruning dwarf trees is basically the same as pruning full-sized or standard trees, only on a smaller scale, except where your plan is espaliering (training trees on a trellis).

Do not prune fruit trees the first year after planting, except for the initial pruning done at the nursery.

When pruning, remember that, contrary to the popular belief that the bottom branches go up as the tree grows, the distance from the ground to the first branch never alters. The old, neglected fruit tree that hasn't seen a pruner for years may be brought back to a controlled growth if you do it gradually.

The urge may be to really hack and chop the tree so as to clean it in one operation, but the result of that will be a mass of water shoots.

With old trees cut out the branches that cross through the tree or over one another. Heavy branches that grow from the trunk at a sharp angle should be cabled. Where there are two the same size growing in a Y-shape, one should be cut back part way to maintain an unequal balance to avoid an eventual splitting.

Long limbs that end in numerous branches should be thinned to lighten the load.

Large cuts should be slanted and coated with tree paint to keep out the insects and moisture until the wounds heal. Branches should be cut flush with other branches without leaving stubs.

A handy pruning time guide

Peach, plum, and cherry trees These trees generally require little pruning, except for shaping or training, or when branches become congested.

Raspberry, blackberry, loganberry vines Vines should have all the wood that has fruited removed, leaving only the strongest young shoots for next year. This pruning must be done after fruiting.

Rose bushes Cut out the weak wood and prune back to about 8 inches (20 centimeters) in early spring.

Climbing roses Cut out only the weak and dead wood and tip back remaining wood to shape.

Flowering shrubs that bloom before June Prune as soon as flowering is finished, cutting back dead and diseased wood and those branches that have flowered.

Flowering shrubs that bloom after June   Prune in early spring, removing dead or weak wood and cutting back if required.

Broadleaf evergreens   Cut back after blooming, usually in May or June.

Conifer evergreens   Prune and shape in May or June.

Spray all your shrubs and trees at this time of year with a formula of lime sulphur and dormant oil, following the directions on the container and assuring the spray is put on with as much pressure as possible. This demands the use of a good sprayer. Do this in late winter or early spring, and for best results, right after pruning.

The love you give plants will be returned many times

One can get addicted to plants, and I've got the bug! Plants bring much beauty and pleasure indoors or outdoors, to man or woman, rich or poor.

Plants were once my whole life, apart from family and friends, but now I am too often tied up with desk work and meetings at the Parliament Buildings where I'm often stared at in bewilderment as I go about a meeting room, checking the plants for water and food, and picking off dead leaves.

A lot of people don't realize that if you love a plant, it will love you back. Plants respond to good treatment, a kind word, some tepid tea, and the sound of good music—even a happy relationship between family members shows up in plant growth.

We all know that a pleasant, kindly grandmother grows the best African violets and can also produce a mini-crop of old-fashioned herbs for her favorite recipes. I have noticed that often big families and older-type homes have the greatest window gardens and the most productive kitchen plots, whereas those poor plants in bare and cold-looking modern offices drop their leaves.

Many commercial organizations, particularly cucumber and

tomato growers in the United States, are now experimenting with soft classical music in the greenhouses, and the initial results appear to be bigger and better crops.

As part of our "get acquainted with the plant world" effort, which requires my writing and your reading, we'll need to clearly understand that plants are living creatures with feelings and understandings.

Plants have long been distinguished from animals, in part by not having the power of movement. There are still those who'll claim that animals have brains and instincts, while plants do not. This is entirely wrong. Plants have feelings, instinct, and, yes, even a brainlike sensory organ we call roots.

A recent experiment in New York where a lie detector measuring device was attached to a philodendron plant concluded that plants respond positively to soft, quality music and kind words expressed in a soft voice, while they act negatively when cursed at or surrounded by harsh, loud music. The polygraph (lie detector) needle jumped frantically when the plant was subjected to a bawling out.

A flower bulb, when planted, even upside down, will always send its roots downwards. Even when the bulb is allowed to root out of the soil the roots will still grow in the direction of the soil, regardless of how the bulb is pointed or how far it is from the soil.

Put a plant in a box in a dark closet with a small light bulb at the base of the box and watch even the sturdiest plant grow right down the side of the box to reach the light.

Have you ever noticed how the tendrils on a climbing plant will continue to revolve in search of support even when the support isn't there?

Plants are smart, as I'll continue to demonstrate, and valuable, too. You can live completely on vegetables and be pretty healthy, but you would perish on a straight meat diet.

Moisture needs of your plants can vary a lot

Plants vary in their moisture needs, ranging from those which want to be on the dry side to those which need very moist conditions. You should learn what the plant's moisture requirements are, so you should ask at the time of purchase, buy booklets featuring your selected plants, or learn from experience by close observation.

For those plants preferring dryness, do not water until the soil feels very dry quite deep in the pot and the pot begins to feel light. For those plants which need to be slightly moist, water if the soil starts to dry but is not yet completely dry. For those which need to be very moist, water thoroughly before any sign of dryness shows.

Some plants and the condition they need

Dry side   Chinese evergreen, cactus, bromeliads, succulents, sansevieria, prayer plant, peperomia.

Moist side   Zebra plant, neanthe bella palm, coleus, nephthytis, table fern, staghorn fern, piggy back, wandering Jew, asparagus fern.

Slightly moist   Aluminum plant, baby tears, gloxinia, pellionia, Boston fern, fiddleleaf fig, false aralia, lipstick, begonia, spider plant, grape ivy, crofton, creeping Charlie, philodendron, ivy, African violet, weeping fig.

You may want to follow this general rule as for watering. Test the soil by putting your finger in it. With smaller pots, if the top half-inch or three-quarter-inch of the soil is dry, water. With bigger pots, if dry one to two inches into pot, water. With hanging baskets, take out of the macrame or away from the hanger and place in the sink to water, allowing water to drain through properly and completely before hanging up again.

Most of the problems affecting houseplants are the result of improper watering practices.

The two that give the most trouble are overwatering and lack of sufficient drainage. The two are identical—unhealthy plants with yellowing leaves.

It is often more harmful to keep plants too wet than not wet enough. Excessive moisture in the root area fills up the air cells, depriving roots of the necessary oxygen. Plants must have water to live, but don't drown them.

The amount of water depends on the prevailing temperature, humidity, size of the pot, and plant. Generally speaking, larger plants need more water than smaller ones; heavy-foliaged plants need more water then lighter ones; plants in smaller conatiners in sunlight need more than those in larger container in less light. The water used should be tepid, preferably about room temperature. Extreme temperatures cause shock.

Beware of the red spider mite

Almost anywhere you drive in our region you see spruce trees—Colorado, Alberta, blue spruce, and dwarf spruce—that appear to be dying. Some years are particularly bad because of mild winter weather and dry spells in late winter and very early spring, which are ideal for the red spider mite. Many trees everywhere are badly infested.

The mite is so small that you can not see the pest with the naked eye. You can, however, often see the small spider webs, especially when the tree is covered in dew.

The earliest evidence of red spider is the purple tinge of the needles before they turn completely brown and drop off. The first part of the tree or shrub to brown is that nearest the inside, where it is also driest, and from there it works to the outside.

The spider mite likes it dry, which is also why plants indoors are more subject to attack when the plants are dry. The spider mite will in time completely defoliate and kill the trees if these horrible insects are left unchecked. Spruce trees should really be sprayed both in spring and late fall with Lagon, Orthene, or a similar product. If you see evidence of red spider mite damage, the trees must be sprayed immediately to prevent total damage and stop the spread of the mites to other trees, shrubs, and plants in the garden or indoors.

Pesticides should be used with great care

I've written several articles on the alternatives to pesticides. We can not eliminate the use of pesticides completely, since a healthy garden requires you to keep ahead of insects and disease, but there are ways of minimizing their use.

When you must spray, use a small sprayer if possible. Companion planting is becoming more and more popular, and often eliminates the need for extensive pesticide treatments.

Pesticides must be properly used and stored. Here are some general rules for their safe and effective use.

Use the right pesticide. Resist the temptation to use whatever happens to be on your garage shelf unless you can identify it as the right insecticide for the job.

Read the label. Do exactly what the instructions say. Natural human tendency is to reason, "If two tablespoons per gallon are recommended then surely four will be twice as effective." That's not the case. All the reasoning does is double the garden expenses and, carried to an extreme, causes ecological, environmental, and even toxicological problems. By following the instructions closely, measuring, and observing all the warnings on the label, you will ensure that your garden chemicals perform their assigned task efficiently and safely.

Mix only the amount of spray needed at a given time. Spray that is left over or diluted should not be stored. It is only wasted and can cause disposal problems.

Always, always make sure containers are stored well out of reach of children and pets.

Insecticides and their application

Insect-contact insecticides are used for sap-sucking insects such as greenfly or aphids.

Leaf-contact insecticides for plant-chewing insects such as

caterpillars, work by coating the insects' source of food. You do not have to hit the insect, but you must obtain good cover of the leaves.

Systemic insecticides for sap-sucking or chewing insects work inside the plant in the sap stream. Even new growth after treatment is protected, hidden insects killed, and beneficial insects spared. The systemic is available in a fertilizer combination, which can simply be sprinkled about the roots and watered, or in the liquid form, which can be brushed on the bottom of the stems or sprayed on.

Fungicides are used to control diseases. They are generally used to prevent, not cure, attack. Benomyl and Funginex, which are systemic, may be exceptions. Fungicides should be applied before the disease takes hold.

Herbicides or weedkillers are available in three basic forms. Products like Pre-emerge are applied on freshly cultivated soil and prevent the weeds from sprouting. This type is particularly effective around established shrubs or plants. Selective weedkillers are those used most often on the lawns. The types of weeds killed are dependent upon the product you choose. Soil sterilant "kills it all" and is most commonly used on driveways or along fencelines.

I prefer the products which are organic in nature, but chemicals are still very much in use. More research and increased competition among manufacturers will, in time, produce many new and better products.

Prune those roses now

There's still time to prune the roses if you haven't already done so during the past few weeks.

A rose bush, unlike a tree or flowering bush, does not grow by producing shoots that continue to increase in size every year for as long as the plant lives. Rose stems grow actively and bear flowers for only a few years, after which the upper portions become exhausted. New shoots then appear from buds lower down on the stems, and the parts above the new shoot die. This means that a rose bush left unpruned becomes a tangled and shapeless mass of live and dead wood, with small and poor-quality blooms borne on weak, thin shoots. The purpose of pruning is to get rid of the old and dead wood every year and encourage the regular development of new strong and healthy stems.

Feeding, not pruning, will give you more flowers next year, but pruning will give you a well-shaped bush or tree that will continue to flower freely for many years to come.

To prune bush roses, cut out completely all dead wood and parts of stems that are obviously diseased or damaged. Remove completely all the suckers coming from below the bud union that is at soil level. Cut out completely all the very thin stems, and remove any branch that rubs against another. Aim to produce an open-centered bush. After having removed all but the healthy and ripe stems, prune these back to about 8 inches (20 centimeters) above the bud union.

Miniature and shrub roses require very little pruning. Remove dead or sick wood and trim to shape if necessary. Climbing roses also require very little pruning apart from the removal of dead or tired wood. The main stems are left much intact, but the small lateral branches should be reduced to about 3 inches (7 centimeters).

Feed your roses now too

This is a good time to give your rose bushes a feeding of rose food. The rose food contains sufficient quantities of nitrogen, phosphate, and potash, as well as other minor elements, to get them off to a good start before summer.

If you're planting new rose bushes, remember to provide good drainage and good soil. Keep them away from areas where the roots of trees or fast-growing hedges are prevalent. Roses need sun and should get at least four hours. Sun filtered through trees is usually sufficient.

Hybrid tea roses should be planted by themselves in a bed or border so air can circulate through them. Climbers must be tied to a wall, trellis, or pole. *Floribundas* and *grandifloras* are most versatile and will grow almost anywhere.

In the April chapter you'll find more information on rose varieties and their care.

Lawns pay great dividends in pleasures received

The most important part of our garden or outdoor living area may well be the lawn.

Nothing feels as good to your bare feet; nothing else will ever be as great for wrestling on or playing badminton and croquet on; nothing else offers the plain joy of turning somersaults. There's nothing that looks as good, is as soft, as resilient, can be raked away so easily, yet allows water and oxygen in to feed the tree and shrub roots below its surface. So let's keep it that way.

Mowing is no longer the chore it used to be, and the result of a finished job—a neat, trim, and tidy lawn—makes body and soul feel great.

How to make a lawn

Let's take a simple trip through the steps and throw in a few tips worth remembering.

When preparing the soil for a new lawn, work it well to a depth of at least 5 inches (13 centimeters) and rake out weeds, stones, and other debris. There's no better time to do this than in the initial preparation.

If your soil is sandy, work in some organic matter and blend it into existing soil to develop a transitional layer. Check your soil for acidity (pH), and, if it is below 5.5, work into the soil about 50 pound (25 kilograms) of white agricultural lime to ever 1000 to 1500 square feet (100 to 150 square meters) of lawn area. Install irrigation if desired.

If you are using imported topsoil, take half the amount you are going to need and spade it into existing soil to make an even mix.

Then add the rest of the top soil to bring it to the desired level.

Now comes the job of levelling. Use a drag (my favorite is a "window frame"—four timbers in a square frame with a weight on top of it). When pulled horizontally along loose soil, this will pick up a high spot and put it in a low area. You can finish it off with a straight edge or rake.

If you still want to perfect it, roll in two directions with a heavy roller.

Now mix 10 pounds (4.5 kilograms) of your selected grass seed thoroughly with 40 pounds (20 kilograms) of organic fertilizer and sprinkle evenly to about 1500 square feet (150 square meters). The most popular grass mixes are Blacklawn (Special Mix), Frontlawn (Deluxe Mix), Shady lawn or Fabulawn (drought resistant, beautiful, and tough.

After seeding, rake gently to lightly put the seed and fertilizer in better contact with the soil; then water as required to keep at least the top one inch of soil slightly moist at all times.

Mow the lawn for the first time when the grass blades begin to take on a definite curvature—usually when 2 inches (5 centimeters) high—and use a sharp mower.

An established lawn

Your lawn may require reseeding. *Do not* reseed if the trouble that caused the need for renovation is a basic fault. If there's basic trouble, renovating will probably only promote the same headaches at the same time next year.

But if you have lost a part or even an entire lawn from what you are reasonably sure is an outside factor (such as lawn moth, leatherjackets, disease, long drought and, yes, often a heavy moss infestation), and if the lawn is still approximately as level and smooth as you want it to be, reseed as follows.

Mow what is left of the old lawn thoroughly and closely.

Rake up the clippings and scrape away at the old turf

surface with a hard steel rake.

Go over the lawn again with the mower to cut off the runners you've exposed. Pull the weeds and rake again.

Loosen the soil mechanically or with a fork. Cut off any humps and fill in the low spots.

Cover seed with a light sprinkling of fine peat moss, and water very well and regularly.

Remember that this method can be applied to an entire lawn. Normally, however, when that much renovation is required you would follow the new lawn process. Reseeding, therefore, is generally used to bring an existing lawn up to the desired standard or to restore a good grass sod in bare areas or spots.

Beautiful summer lawns require labor in March

To have a beautiful lawn next summer, start today. The warm days of spring give us our first opportunity to survey the lawn and check for winter damage or weaknesses. A common problem in some northwest climates is the green moss that appears among the grass blades. This usually is an indication of low soil fertility, high acidity, too much shade, or too much moisture. Regular fertilizing may solve the problem. The grass will grow stronger, and moss very often fades out in a rich soil.

Moss in the lawn under trees is usually the result of too much shade, plus low fertility because of root competition. Apply twice the usual amount of fertilizer to these areas.

The best all-round fertilizers to apply from now until fall are numbered on the bag 13-5-7, 10-6-4, or 12-6-8, and these fertilizers contain four sources of nitrogen and iron for a long-lasting effect.

In areas where shade continues to be a problem, rake the area hard with a steel rake and sprinkle a generous amount of seed specially bred for shady areas. Cover the seed with a fine sprinkling of peat moss and sand.

In the deepest shade where only the moss will grow, don't fight it. Use it to your advantage and plant a beautiful shade-loving groundcover such as ajuga, pachysandra, periwinkle, or gualtheria.

No amount of fertilizer will help if the soil is too acid, and in our climate after a long wet season, acidity is a prevalent problem. The rule of thumb says we must apply white lime to the lawn at least once per year at the rate of 50 pounds to every 1000 to 1500 square feet (25 kilograms to every 100 to 150 square meters) of lawn, and now is the time to do it. If you use the cheaper gray lime, triple the quantity. It is preferable to apply lime two weeks before fertilizing.

To eliminate the moss quickly, you may use a moss killer fertilizer at the rate or 40 to 50 pounds for 3000 square feet (20 to 25 kilograms for 300 square meters), but it must be applied on a warm day with a least 48 hours of sunshine to follow.

When moss growth is caused by water standing on the soil or in the top layer of soil, dig up those spots and mix in peat or manure; then reseed. If the drainage is bad, install underground drain tiles.

Your lawn is probably ready for that first cutting. Debates about how high to cut the grass for the ideal are immaterial, because what is low for one type of grass may be high for another. If you have an area of bent grass, anything over one inch (2.5 centimeters) would eventually kill it; yet anything less than 1½ inches (4 centimeters) would wipe out a Kentucky blue grass lawn—worse still if both types of grass are in your lawn. For our area, however, the rule of thumb is 1½ inches (4 centimeters).

Try not to weaken the growth of your lawn through irregular cutting. Cut often enough so that you are taking off no more than about one-third of the grass blade. I prefer to remove the clippings so they do not mat or make a tight thatch, which could be an invitation to disease. The best thing to do with your clippings is to compost them as directed in the June chapter.

Finally, check your lawn for leatherjackets. Look below the sod. If there are gray-looking grubs about 1 inch (2.5 centimeters) long, you'll need to spray with Diazinon, 2 tablespoons per gallon (4 ml per 4 liters) of water for every 200 square feet (20 square meters). If you don't, they'll eat the grass roots, and your lawn could turn to a mud field before your eyes.

I keep telling my gardening friends that it's a lot better to use a watering can with a liquid mix weedkiller, applying it directly to the weeds, than to spread the poison over the entire lawn whether it needs it or not, as is done with some weedkillers. A good fertilizer plus direct application of poisons only when necessary, will be more effective in the long run, and is healthier for lawn structure.

This recommendation assures better and safer control for less money, and you'll keep all that poison out of the compost box if you're collecting clippings.

More on lawns in the June chapter. Lawn care is an ongoing process and almost a 12-month process in coastal areas.

Lime, the oldest and best soil conditioner

The most popular product in the garden centers these days is agriculture lime.

Lime is especially important in our region. I would like to list some of the reasons and the benefits of liming in order to give you a better understanding.

Rain steadily washes lime out of the soil at an annual average rate of 1 pound per 32 square yards (0.03 liter per square meter). Slowly the land becomes sour, and neither manure nor most fertilizers are of any help in correcting this condition.

The answer is to apply lime, the oldest and still the best soil conditioner. Lime neutralizes sourness. A very small number of plants grow well in sour soils.

Lime brings life into the soil. When soils are sour, beneficial bacteria and earthworms tend to die out. Lime helps them to survive.

Lime breaks up heavy clay soils. It brings the tiny clay particles together into crumbs, making heavy soils easier to work with, warmer, and better draining.

Try proving to yourself the property of lime. Add a teaspoonful (5 ml) of clay to a glass of water and stir until it is all in suspension. When you stop stirring the liquid will remain muddy because the minute particles of clay are not heavy enough to fall to the bottom of the glass.

Now stir in ¼ teaspoon (1 ml) of lime. The clay particles group together into clearly visible soil crumbs, which quickly sink to the bottom of the glass.

Lime is a plant food. Calcium, the main component of lime, is a necessary food for all plants. Lime makes other plant foods available. It acts on humus, setting free the elements needed for healthy plant growth.

Lime discourages pests. Some soil diseases, such as cabbage club root, are checked by liming. Soil pests such as slugs, leatherjackets, and wireworms avoid limed soils. Give them a good diet of lime and spoil their summer while you spare your lawn.

Clematis pruning time

I'm asked time and again about the pruning of clematis vines. Left unpruned, most clematis develop into tangled masses of growth, bearing their flowers high above the bare, woody stems. The technique is to prune to provide the greatest amount of coverage and the greatest display of bloom.

Pruning at planting is important but is often overlooked. Many clematis, particularly the large-flowered hybrids, will tend to grow rapidly upwards on a single stem during the first season after planting unless pinched at an early stage.

At planting, the stem should be cut back to the lowest pair of strong buds to encourage the plant to produce further bottom growth.

This initial pruning applies to all clematis, whether planted while completely dormant in very early spring or later when in leaf. It appears complicated, but really clematis can be divided into three categories for pruning reference, based on age of the growth on which the flowers are produced.

The first group flower only on the current year's growth; the second group, a number of spring flowering varieties or species, produce all their blooms on new shoots from the previous year's wood; a third group, which includes many well-known hybrids such as Nelly Moser, produce flowers from last season's growth during early summer and a further display of small flowers in later summer and fall from the current year's young shoots.

The first group comprises all the clematis species and hybrids that flower in summer and fall entirely on the new growth produced during the current season. If left unpruned, they begin growth in the spring from where they flowered the previous season and quickly become bare at the base with flowers at the top only.

Pruning is very simple and consists of cutting back all the previous year's growth virtually to ground level, which I signalled you to do at the end of the February chapter. The pruning cuts should be made immediately above the lowest pair of strong buds on each stem.

Varieties or species in this group are *Clematis orientalis, Clematis tangutica, Clematis texensis,* and, the most popular of the large-flowered hybrids, *Clematis jackmanii.*

The second group consists mainly of vigorous spring flowering species, which flower between April and June on short shoots from growth produced the previous summer.

Examples include *Clematis montana, Clematis chryscoma, Clematis aplina,* and *Clematis macropetala.*

The first two species, as mentioned earlier, are very rapid growers. These are merely sheared to keep them tidy until they require rejuvenation. This can be done by cutting the old stems back hard to within 2 or 3 feet (60 to 90 centimeters) of ground level in early spring. Feed and water well. In a few seasons the clematis should be flowering freely.

During the first two years, pruning at planting and training to form a good framework may be all that's required.

The third and following years, the pruning of mature plants consists of cutting away all the flowered wood to within a few inches of the main framework immediately after flowering.

ROSES

REMOVE DEAD WOOD AND CROSS BRANCHES TO OPEN CENTER FIRST

PRUNE AGAIN IN WINTER TO REMOVE DAMAGED WOOD

WRONG ←   RIGHT ←

PRUNE FLUSH WITH BUD UNION TO ELIMINATE STUBS

CLEMATIS

PRUNE FOR HORIZONTAL GROWTH ←

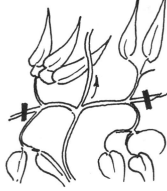

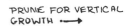

PRUNE FOR VERTICAL GROWTH •→

This stimulates vigorous, long growth that can be trained or guided as required, or allowed to cascade naturally. This growth will provide next season's flowering display, and must not be winter pruned.

The third group contains all the hybrids that provide large, exquisite flowers from May to July on the previous year's wood. While the flowers are being produced, shoots from the old wood are being formed. This produces further crops of medium-sized blooms during late summer and early fall.

Popular varieties in this group include Nelly Moser, the President, Mme. le Coutre, and the double-flowered Duchess of Edinburgh.

The growth habit of this group makes them difficult to prune satisfactorily without a good deal of work, and they may be left entirely unpruned or only lightly pruned until they become straggly and out of control.

These strong growers should be trained to prevent tangling. Thin out the weak branches and trim back the vigorous shoot to develop neat, attractive vines. Where two strong growths break from the same joint or those adjoining, pinch out both to prevent one from driving the other into dormancy. In spring when buds are well swollen, trim out all the dead wood but leave it in place as support for new growth.

Never kink a clematis or fasten it with wire.

Q: I had a lovely golden privet hedge which, for the past several years, has turned more green, to the point where it's now almost totally green. Why?
A: Your hedge appears to be in shade and that will do it every time if the shade is too dense. Even in good light there is often a tendency for parts of the shrub to revert to the faster growing, all-green parent form. Cut out such shoots immediately.

Q: My plum tree has a number of brown and warty outgrowths on the branches. What are they and what harm do they do?
A: This is black knot and must be pruned out completely.

Otherwise the tree will lose its vigor and die.

Q: My lovely houseplant has wilted with yellowing leaves and soft stems. Also, some of the leaves are dropping. What have I done that is wrong?
A: You've overwatered. Allow the plant to dry out. Trim off the yellow leaves and water more carefully in the future.

Q: What vegetables are frost-hardy and can be planted now?
A: Beets, broccoli, Brussels sprouts, cabbage, cauliflower, celery, chard, collards, endive, kale, kohlrabi, leeks, lettuce, onions, parsley, peas, potaotes, radishes, spinach, and turnips. Plants, seeds, or sets can be planted now.

Q: I have a very sandy soil. What vegetables can I grow?
A: Sandy soils are not the best for commercial growing, but for home use, mix in a generous amount of mushroom manure and you'll do okay with most vegetables. For leafy vegetables, continue to feed.

Q: I want to grow a vegetable garden this year but my soil is full of weeds and quackgrass. What do I do and what do I grow?
A: Treat the area to be planted with Weedrite. Weedrite will kill most of the weeds and grasses, and you can cultivate and prepare the soil for planting within 7 to 10 days. Try your favorite vegetables, as I'm not aware of your soil condition. Time will tell about further measures you will need for the selection you make.

Q: Our trees and shrubs are often bothered by mice and rabbits. Which tree will the rabbits leave alone?
A: Try a Paul's scarlet hawthorn tree.

Q: We have a thick-leaved evergreen magnolia tree that refuses to bloom. What's wrong?
A: Nothing. You have a southern magnolia and they'll often take a dozen years before they bloom.

Q: **Should I cut the runners off my strawberry plants?**
A: The production of runners by strawberry plants is perfectly natural. The severe competition from overcrowding is the reason for removing runner plants. The plants should be kept properly spaced. Remove excess runners at the first opportunity in spring and continue to do so every two to three weeks.

Q: **Can I use Weed-and-Feed fertilizer on my lawn now?**
A: It's a bit early yet. I would wait until the weather warms.

Q: **How large should seedlings be before transplanting?**
A: Seedlings should be transplanted as soon as they form their first true leaves (these are the third and fourth leaves that form) and before they become overcrowded in the flat.

Q: **What is meant by acid soil?**
A: One in which the chemical reaction is acidic instead of alkaline, as measured by the pH scale. This scale corresponds, in a way, to the thermometer for measuring temperature.

Q: **What is oyster scale? What damage does it do and how can I control it?**
A: It's a suckling insect that forms a hard, circular covering (resembles the shape of lady bug) that covers branches of trees. They most often attack maple and fruit trees, but if the infestation is bad enough they'll get into many other trees and shrubs. It may kill young trees in two or three years. You may still spray now in March with dormant oil and lime sulphur, but once leaf buds begin to break, use malathion or other recommended insecticides with a small amount of oil to help it stick.

Q: **Every year I have trouble with my sweet black cherry tree. The cherries form and then when they are the size of peas, they all fall off. What is the problem and what do I do?**
A: There are several possible reasons for this, though I suspect it's the first in my list of three possible causes. Lack of pollination—if there is no other cherry tree of another variety

nearby, then the tree is not properly pollinated. Plant another cherry tree, preferably a sour pie cherry in this case. It could be injury by plum curculios, which attack the small fruit. The best control is spraying just after the petals fall with methoxychlor or malathion. Lack of iron in the soil is common in the region because it tends to wash out with all the rains. This can be corrected by applying iron chelates around the tree in early spring before the sap begins to run. Punch holes 1 foot (0.3 meter) deep with a tire iron, about 3 feet (1 meter) apart in a circle about two-thirds of the way out from the trunk and the tips of the branches. Good luck.

Q: What kind of soil is needed for peach trees?
A: Any good soil that is well drained. They prefer sandy loam, however.

Q: Can bearing-size fruit trees be purchased at a nursery?
A: Bearing-age trees may be the nursery's leftovers that were not large enough to sell at 1 or 2 years of age. They experience such a shock from moving that they are not likely to bear much, if any, fruit before the 2-year-old would, unless it was container grown. Container-grown apples will often bear the first year.

Q: What soil is best for carrots? Do I feed, and how often should I plant?
A: You need well-limed and aerated sandy loam soil. Use plenty of humus and 4-10-10 fertilizer. Make three carrot plantings: early spring, early summer, and midsummer (early August). This way you'll have a succession of crops.

Q: I cannot raise cabbage or cauliflower in my garden. Why?
A: If soil is not poor, it may be infested with club root, which attacks cabbage and cauliflower. Try new soil in a different part of the garden. Dig to a depth of twelve inches; use plenty of rotted manure. Cultivate frequently, water during dry spells, and side dress with a good fertilizer.

Q: **What kind of plant food should I give my gardenia?**
A: A 4-12-4 fertilizer is recommended. Particularly suited are fertilizers that provide nitrogen in the form of ammonia such as tankage, dried blood, and sulphate of ammonia.

Q: **When is the best time to divide and replant an old Boston fern?**
A: In the spring, just as a new growth is begining. Select younger and stronger crowns from the outside of the plant for replanting rather than the old, woody interior parts.

Q: **I noticed swellings on the roots of my roses when transplanting them. What shall I do about this?**
A: This is crown gall, a bacterial disease that is soil-borne as well as plant-borne. It gradually weakens and kills the plant. Take the plant out, prune out all the galls, and dip remaining roots in a solution of 4 tablespoons of Captan per gallon (4 liters) of water. Then plant in a new area or in sterilized soil.

April

Prune now for bigger, better berries

I hope by now you've pruned your fruit trees, ornamental trees, and vines.

The evergreens come later, but given the first few days of good weather, you should immediately take care of the berry bushes. If you want the best and biggest berries, now's the time to prepare.

Gooseberry   Gooseberry bushes are the most difficult to prune.

The first-year pruning consists of cutting back leaders by half in November. The second and following years, the secret is selective thinning. Remove any branches that are crossing, broken, diseased, excessively strong, or obviously worn out.

Be sure to leave shoots spaced sufficiently far apart to permit the entry of a hand to gather the gooseberries. Always cut to a half-inch (1 centimeter) above an upward, inward-pointing bud to prevent the bush from becoming weepy and sprawly.

Red, black, and white currants   Red, black, and white currants are shortened back to about half at planting time. Cut back to outward-pointing buds. In summer shorten any unwanted laterals to about 4 inches (10 centimeters), leaving the leaders untouched.

The following year, repeat the pruning of the leaders, cutting them back by one-half to outward-pointing buds. Shorten the summer pruned laterals to about 1 inch (2.5 centimeters).

Remove all dead, diseased, or damaged wood. The black currant bears on last year's wood, and thus, for them, summer pruning is not recommended.

In the fall, cut out the old fruited canes completely.

Raspberries Raspberries are perennial plants with biennial stems. The aim of pruning is to encourage enough, but not too many, new canes to replace the old ones as they fruit and die. When planting your first canes, cut back to 10 inches (25 centimeters) of ground level. Do not cut any shorter at this stage, as there is a risk that the plant will die.

There will be no fruit the first season. If any flowers appear on the cut-down stumps, they should be removed. New canes will emerge from below ground.

If there are too many produced, something much more likely to occur in later years, the surplus young canes should be thinned out to leave the strongest survivors about 4 inches (10 centimeters) apart. Once the canes are growing well, the 10-inch (25-centimeter) stubs should be cut to ground level.

In the fall, a year or so after planting, a series of strong canes should have appeared. Tie them into a post and wire support, with the top wire 6 feet (2 meters) from the ground.

Each cane should stand separate from its neighbors, approximately 4 inches (10 centimeters) apart. In the second and following years any tips that are obviously weak or have been damaged by winter should be cut back into strong, sound tissue. After this the process is quite simple. The canes that have borne fruit are cut down to ground level as soon as possible after harvest, and the thrusting young canes are tied onto the wire to take their place.

Blueberries Blueberries are pruned to a common-sense minimum. Remember that blueberries grow in an acid soil. Wherever rhododendrons grow, blueberries will also thrive.

The fruit is borne on side shoots; the flowerbuds appear on the previous year's growth. Fruiting becomes irregular unless the bush is regularly manured, fertilized, and pruned.

Pruning essentially consists of thinning the crowded and wornout shoots and branches. The usual approach is to do little if any pruning the first three years after planting.

In future years cut back to ground level some of the previously fruited branches that have become twiggy and thus likely to overcrop. Broken branches, dead shoots, and branches close to the ground are also removed.

Home vegetable growing is fun, and fights inflation, too

Home vegetable growing is a pleasurable pastime and a great therapeutic hobby, but, more than that, it is rapidly becoming the most effective inflation fighter and offers some relief from today's high prices.

Compared to prices of all other commodities, food prices are still relatively low. But the pressure is on, and now is the time for each of us to learn how we can aid in easing the world food shortage by growing something edible—perhaps herbs on a windowsill; tomatoes in apartment bay windows; cucumbers, lettuce, and carrots in window boxes; or vertical gardening on fences.

It is only by careful planning that maximum vegetable yield through continuous cropping can be obtained. Know the possibilities and limitations of a crop, and chart out each plant's desires and needs for the months ahead. With a little forethought and practice, you can triple the production per square foot.

A fairly deep, well-drained, open-structured, fertile soil is needed for good vegetable production. Soil should ideally be prepared sufficiently in advance by turning over and leaving to aerate and weather for as long as possible. Add manure at a rate depending on soil structure, but normally a good big bag (100 pounds or 45 kilograms) of mushroom (or horse) manure to every 100 to 150 square feet (10 to 15 square meters) of garden will give your plants plenty to feast on. For acid soils, add enough lime to keep the pH level about 6.5, but do not add lime where you grow the acid-loving crops such as potatoes. Cabbage family members need more lime; white lime also works to minimize clubroot problems.

Soil compacting must be avoided at all times. Lay some planks along the rows of root crops so that ordinary walking and working in the garden doesn't destroy good root development.

All vegetables need moisture throughout the growing season. Too much or too little water can reduce the growing quality. Water must soak down into the soil to a depth of 4 inches (10 centimeters) for beans, cole crops, and other shallow-rooted vegetables; 6 inches (15 centimeters) for vine and root crops, and 8 inches (20 centimeters) for tomatoes. Apply water slowly (try a soaker hose). If soil becomes crusty, cultivate to permit water and air circulation. A strip of burlap over the newly seeded row will prevent soil splash, keep seeds in place, and hold moisture in. Remove the burlap as soon as the seeds begin to establish themselves. Remember, it's preferable to water in the morning.

There are many different ways to increase production, but consider these few suggestions.

Plant different varieties of a single crop. For example, when planting sweet corn, plant both an early and a late variety. You will extend the harvest season from three weeks to nine weeks by using different varieties.

You can intercrop. Plant fast-growing early crops between slow-growing late crops, or tall-growing plants between short plants, provided their time for maturing is about the same. Some examples: Leaf lettuce between broccoli (the leaf lettuce will be gone before the broccoli matures); radishes between beans; sweet carrots next to peas. Using the intercropping method, we can plant much closer than normally, not only using the available space to greatest advantage but also cutting down on the tedious task of weeding.

Remember that a border of marigolds around the garden will trap any nematodes.

When planting your vegetables, mix 4-10-10 flower and vegetable food in with the soil, and, during the growing season, use the popular Feed-All (7-7-7) or an all-purpose 6-8-6 fertilizer.

Don't let your ground lie fallow in the growing season. Reap the benefits of succession or continuous planting. Short-maturing crops are followed by long-maturing crops, or long by short; root crops by leaf crops; or fruiting crops (beans, etc.) by root crops. It is important that the replacement be an alternate crop requiring different nutrients. This also helps control insects and diseases.

In late fall, it is important to dig the soil early.The longer the soil lies fallow, the better.

Always buy good seeds and plants. Store your seed packets inside a tightly-lidded tin in your fridge. They'll keep better and for a longer period of time. When purchasing seedling plants instead of sowing your own, choose sturdy, green plants with good root systems. There must be a minimum delay between buying and planting.

Rotate your crops. You should not grow a vegetable in the same spot year after year. If you do, soil troubles will build up and the level of nutrients will become unbalanced in the soil. Changing your plantings is the solution. The simplest plan to follow is roots this year, an above-ground crop next year, and then back to a root crop.

Soil and weather conditions determine the best time for planting. The soil must be moist but not wet and waterlogged. Sow seeds in rows; broadcasting them over an area makes weeding too difficult. Mark the ends of the rows with stakes, and remember the basic seeding rules—not too early, not too deeply, not too thickly!

Thin promptly to ensure rapid growth. Remove the weeds and thin the seedlings as soon after germination as possible. Overcrowding at this early stage can be crippling.

Firm the plants after thinning and gently water to settle the disturbed roots.

Tenderness and flavor in leaf crops and many root crops depend upon rapid growth. Ensure that the plants receive adequate water and nutrients.

Many vegetables, such as lettuce, celery, and cabbage, can not be kept or stored for later use. To avoid gluts and shortages, sow a short row of vegetables every few weeks. Many vegetable varieties are ready for eating in as little as one or two months; thus you can plant again and again. I have picked lettuce as late as November and onions as late as January.

Pick most crops early and often. You may be surprised to find that vegetables can be and are often best harvested at different stages.

Some of the tastiest turnip meals are from pickings not much bigger than the size of a golfball, and if you want sweet, tasty carrots, try picking them when they reach finger length. These are the times of peak flavor and tenderness; you'll not get them in stores that way because the growers do not find it economical.

Some crops, such as cucumbers, peas, and beans, should be picked regularly, as just a few mature fruits or pods left on the plant can bring cropping to an end.

Again, remember to keep out the weeds. Weeds rob the plants of water, food, space, and light, and become breeding grounds for pests.

There are times when a spray or some other chemical treatment may be necessary for pests. Consult your licensed pesticide dispenser at a nursery to advise you on which one to use.

Inspect plants regularly to keep ahead of problems. Before spraying, read the instructions, and avoid using too little or too much. Apply a fine, drenching spray above and below the leaves. After spraying, don't forget to wash out the sprayer. Do not keep the liquid for use next week. Get rid of badly infected plants. Do not leave the sources of infection in the garden.

Many plant troubles are caused by incorrect feeding and soil moisture problems. Use Flower and Vegetable 4-10-10 fertilizer in order to avoid soft growth.

Never let the roots get dry, but daily sprinklings instead of a good soaking will do more harm than good.

Fifteen great vegetables for your garden

By now you know many of the basics and also some of the specifics about the favorite vegetables for backyard gardens. It's a bit too early for tomatoes and cucumbers, as they really should not go outside yet. More about these two great favorites in the May chapter.

Knowing what to grow and where to grow it, considering soil, sun, water, and circumstances, can easily increase total yields by one hundred percent.

Celery You'll need only 1/32 of an ounce (about a gram) for about 100 plants. A 30-foot (9-meter) row will produce 40 pounds (20 kilograms). Time between sowing and picking is normally about five months, but buying plants instead of starting from seed can save you at least one month and will allow you to plant much earlier. Start seeds indoors in April and plant out in May and June. Place plants 8 inches (20 centimeters) apart, in squares instead of rows, so that plants may shade each other. In August, pull soil up against plants. Plant in a sunny area in rich soil, and feed and water regularly.

Lettuce For a 30-foot (9-meter) row use 1/8 of an ounce (3.5 grams) of seeds. You can also get the plants ready grown. It takes only twelve weeks to harvest time. For a summer crop, sow outdoors in March, April, May, or June. For an early winter crop sow in August, but cover plants with hot caps during October and November. For a spring crop, sow a hardy variety in early September, but protect over winter. The soil must contain plenty of organic matter and must not be acid. Water and feed regularly and rake in Diazinon granules if pests are a problem. Lift your plants as soon as a firm heart has formed. Try leaf lettuce also. It seems to be as popular as head lettuce in the home garden.

Onions   Onions may be grown from seed or sets. Most people believe that green onions must always be grown from sets or multiplier bulbs, but actually some of the tastiest green salad onions are the thinnings of the seeded bulb varieties. They can also be grown directly from seed. They are white skinned and mild flavored. When growing onions from seed you will need 1/4 ounce (7 grams) for a 30-foot (9-meter) row, and this should yield about 20 to 25 pounds (9 to 10 kilograms). Use a well-manured soil. Rake soil to a fine tilth before sowing. Sow in March or April or get the plants and plant March through May. You will harvest July through September. Thin as soon as possible to 1 or 2 inches (2.5 to 5 centimeters) apart, and dispose of thinnings. Thin in the evening and after watering. Firm soil after thinning. Thin again when onion tops can be used for greens, and then thin to 5 to 6 inches (13 to 15 centimeters) apart. Break off any flower stems that may appear. Stop watering once the onions have swollen and let the sun ripen them. Dig after foliage dies. Onions grown from sets are not as fussy as from soil—they're much tougher. Firm soil after planting, but plant sets just slightly below surface.

Parsnips   Use 1/4 ounce (7 grams) for a 30-foot (9-meter) row. Yield will be about 30 pounds (15 kilograms). Grow in well-manured soil. Sow outdoors in March through April. Thin after planting but dispose of thinnings. Sow in rows of about 3 seeds every 6 inches (15 centimeters), then thin to one later. The roots are ready to lift when foliage dies in fall. Flavor improves after frost. Lift the roots as required right into winter. If you wish to store some roots for winter, dig roots and place between layers of dry sand or peat in a sturdy box and store in a shed, cool basement, or garage.

Peas   Five hundred seeds per 30-foot (9-meter) row will yield about 30 pounds (15 kilograms). Choose an area where no peas have been grown for the past several years. Use a good organic and manured soil, and apply 4-10-10 fertilizer before seeding. Protect the rows from birds with netting or similar protective covering before seeds germinate. Sow in April, May, or June and harvest July, August, or September. When plants are 3 inches (8 centimeters) high, place some twigs alongside for support. For taller varieties, provide further netting or a trellis support shortly after. Water during dry spells. Spray after flowering if needed for insects. Pick regularly; when pods are left to mature, cropping stops.

Potatoes   Use 5 pounds (2 kilograms) of seed for a 30-foot (9-meter) row to yield 65 pounds (30 kilograms). Plant in April or May. Harvest early varieties in July, midseason varieties in August, and late varieties in September or October. Grow in almost any soil, even in wasteland. Do not use lime. Apply Diazinon granules when planting to prevent wireworm. Plant about 12 inches (30 centimeters) apart. Earth-up the soil when the plant is about 9 inches (22 centimeters) high. In summer use potato dust to prevent blight. Water during dry weather. Begin to dig after flowering, but dig only as needed.

Radish   Radishes take only three to four weeks from sowing to harvest. Sow throughout the summer. Use well-drained soil. Apply 4-10-10 fertilizer before sowing.

Spinach   Summer spinach has round seed, and winter spinach has prickly seed. Sow in rich, organic soil. Sow in April, May, or June for summer variety, or in August or September for winter type. It takes about two months to harvest time. You can have spinach from the garden the year round.

Corn   Every garden must have some, and sowing different varieties that mature at different times can give you sweet corn on the cob all fall.

Bill with scarlet runner beans as tall as a house.

Broad beans You'll need fifty beans for a 15-foot (4.5-meter) double row. Discard any seed with small, round holes. Sow in March and April, and pick in July and August. Yield per 14-foot (4.5-meter) row is about 20 pounds (9 kilograms). Broad beans prefer a fairly rich and well drained soil. Pinch off top 3 inches (8 centimeters) of stem as soon as first beans begin to form. This will give an earlier harvest and help control black fly. Hoe regularly and keep well watered. You can pick them as baby pods 2 inches (5 centimeters) long and cook whole like a French bean, or you can pick when pods are plump but not overripe. Great for freezing.

Regular beans   You'll need about 150 seeds for a 30-foot (9-meter) row. Sow in April, May, and June, and pick in July, August, September, and October. It only takes twelve weeks from sowing to picking. Yield per 30-foot (9-meter) row for the dwarf variety is about 20 pounds (9 kilograms), and for the climbing variety, 30 pounds (14 kilograms). Grow in almost any soil, although regular beans prefer manured soil, and fertilizer (4-10-10) should be applied before sowing. Hoe regularly and water during dry weather, but especially when flowers begin to appear. Begin picking when pods are 4 inches (10 centimeters) long. A pod is ready when it snaps easily when bent. Pick several times a week; the yield may continue from five to eight weeks. Great for freezing, but may also be dried.

Runner beans   You'll need seventy-five seeds for a double 15-foot (4.5-meter) row. Sow April, May, or June. It takes only twelve weeks from sowing to picking. The yield per 15-foot (4.5 meter) row is about 100 pounds (45 kilograms). Choose a sheltered spot with well-manured soil. Fertilizer (4-10-10) should be applied just before sowing. Tie young plants loosely to support, and protect from slugs. Hoe and water regularly. Pinch the tips when plants reach the top of your supports, and spray regularly with water when flowers begin to form; this improves the crop. Harvest over several months, but pick the pods before the beans begin to swell. If pods are allowed to ripen, the plants will cease to yield. Good for freezing also.

Beets   For a 30-foot (9-meter) row, use ¼ ounce (7 grams) of seed. Sow in April, May, and even in June. There are nine to sixteen weeks of harvest depending upon the variety (early or late). It is best to plant some of each. Beets prefer well-fertilized, organic soil; use 4-10-10 fertilizer. Thin out seedlings so that each plant stands singly. Regular watering is essential; dryness will make plants bolt (go to seed), and too much moisture will cause beets to split. You can start harvesting even small, tender beets, but, when doing so, take out every other one, leaving added room for those remaining. When storing beets, twist off tops, leaving about 2 inches (5 centimeters) of stem. Place the beets between layers of dry sand or peat in a sturdy box and store in a shed or garage. The crop will easily keep until March.

Cabbages This group includes broccoli, Brussels sprouts, cabbage, cauliflower, and kale. There are about 8,000 seeds per ounce (28 grams). The seeds germinate in about seven to twelve days, and the yield per plant averages from 1½ to 3 pounds (0.7 to 1.5 kilograms), except for such items as the new apple cabbage, which will go to 11 pounds (5 kilograms) per plant. The time from sowing to harvest depends not only on the type (that is, cauliflower matures much more quickly than broccoli or Brussels sprouts), but also on variety. An early cauliflower matures in three to four months, while a late variety takes up to six months. Time to sow is March or April and May. All brassicas (ornamental cabbage) prefer a rather heavy soil, rich in organic matter. Use plenty of white lime. This helps prevent clubroot. Sprinkle in granular Diazinon when planting cabbage. This helps prevent root fly and cutworm. If seedlings are overcrowded, thin as soon as possible, and put plants in their permanent locations when 3 inches (8 centimeters) high. Leave about 18 inches (46 centimeters) between plants. Plant 1 inch (2.5 centimeters) deeper than they were in the seedbed. Water in well. Water during summer, hoe regularly, feed two or three times with 4-10-10, and use a vegetable dust to keep out bugs when required.

71

Carrots   You'll need about 1/4 ounce (7 grams) for a 30-foot (9-meter) row. Sow from March until July, and pick from one month after sowing until four months after. Yield per 30-foot (9-meter) row is approximately 25 pounds (11 kilograms). The soil must be deep, rich, and somewhat sandy. Do not use manure, but instead sprinkle in 4-10-10 fertilizer, and also use Diazinon granules to help prevent carrot fly and wireworm attacks. Thin out as soon as seedlings are big enough to handle; after that, thin again several times. Now you can harvest delicious little sweet carrots and enjoy your first taste, until the plants are 3 inches apart. Always thin in the evening and after watering. Firm soil after thinning, and do not leave the thinnings on the ground. Water regularly, and remember that rain after a dry spell causes splitting. Carrots may be picked (pulled) as required, and in the fall may be stored in a box just like the beets.

I'm determined to give you the best vegetable garden ever and to encourage everyone to get in the habit of doing our own little bit to fight inflation and encourage good land utilization.

Look for more on vegetables in the May chapter.

Grow your veggies without soil

One of the things most missed by an ever-increasing number of apartment dwellers is the opportunity to go to the backyard, smell the fragrance of the sweet williams, sweet peas, or stocks, pick up on that clean smell of the marigold, nasturtium or calendula, and gather an armful of lettuce, fresh radish, and sweet, crispy carrots only moments before dinner or lunch on the patio.

Even those who have a spacious back yard think they have no choice in winter but to go out and buy the lettuce and other expensive imported salad ingredients for a healthy feast. Yet, with a growing system as old as the pyramids, anyone can grow tender, fresh produce and flavorful herbs the year round.

HYDROPONIC GARDENING

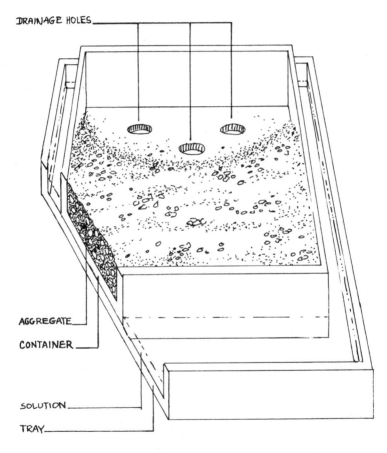

DRAINAGE HOLES

AGGREGATE

CONTAINER

SOLUTION

TRAY

PLANTS ROOTED IN COARSE AGGREGATE IN TOP TRAY
ARE FED NUTRIENT SOLUTION FROM BOTTOM TRAY
THROUGH DRAINAGE HOLES

The ancient system is hydroponics—the art of growing plants in a nutrient water solution instead of soil. The art has been used for quite some time commercially and is receiving increased attention. It is only very recently, however, that hydroponics has become a realistic and successful approach for the home gardener and hobbyist who doesn't have time or space for full-time gardening.

Almost any plant can be grown hydroponically. You can buy a ready-made unit that occupies little more space than a TV set, or you can build your own. For that matter, you can change from fish to vegetables by converting your aquarium to a hydroponic tank that will grow perhaps 50 pounds (25 kilograms) of tomatoes a year in two crops. Lettuce, peppers, onions, and herbs are also good choices for those just starting out.

For the simplest system, all you need is a waterproof container filled with some kind of growing medium or aggregate to support and aerate the roots and provide drainage. The aggregate can be gravel, stones, broken tiles, or, better still, a light-weight porous material, such as vermiculite, perralite, or volcanic rock. Seeds or young plants are placed in the aggregate and fed by a nutrient solution that circulates through it.

A simple fertilizer isn't enough for hydroponic gardening. The nutrient solution must supply all the elements for plant growth. In addition to nitrogen, phosphorous, and potash, there must be at least ten trace elements—sulphur, iron, manganese, zinc, copper, boron, magnesium, calcium, chlorine, and molybdenum. While there are many solutions and formulas, all you really need to worry about is that these elements are present in balanced amounts. Each plant will absorb only what it needs; overfeeding is impossible unless the solution is too strong. There are usually good hydroponic fertilizers ready-mixed and properly balanced available from your local nursery. The only additional feeding is required at the bud development stage when a fertilizer high in phosphorus content should be added.

You will have to watch your solution's pH level. Most vegetables prefer a slightly acid mix—between 5.6 and 6.5. White vinegar will restore a solution that is too alkaline (high pH number). Baking soda will correct one that's too acidic (low pH). The litmus test available at nurseries is the surest way to check.

Two methods are suitable for the circulation of nutrients. One is the flood and drain, in which the growing medium is flooded periodically with the nutrient solution; and the other is a constant flow system that keeps the solution moving steadily through the bottom of the growing medium. A simple timer can be used to activate the pump.

If you want to have success with plenty of lettuce, Tiny Tim tomatoes, herbs, and other leafy vegetables, place your hydroponic garden near window, preferably with a southern or western exposure. If the area is still too dark, add a grow light above your crop to ensure success. Be sure your grow lights do not produce an overly intense amount of heat, especially for the lettuce, radish, and leafy vegetables, as these are basically cool weather plants and too much heat, especially direct heat, will cause a weak and unproductive plant.

Dry air is always a problem in apartments during the winter, but a hydroponic system is a natural humidifier and therefore is beneficial to the entire household—plants and humans alike. Although a relative humidity of forty percent is ideal for both plants and people, it may be more than your home can take in very cold weather without developing condensation problems. Hydroponic greenhouses are also becoming very popular because of the ease of plant maintenance.

Add color and spice to your garden with herbs

Herbs and spices can be some of the most atractive plants in your garden. By using your imagination, you can make herbs a part of the total landscape.

Dwarf sages and thymes make nice borders around flower beds. Rosemary or woolly thyme will cascade beautifully over stone walls. Purple leaf basil or tricolor sage will add a dash of brilliance to an otherwise low-profile corner of your garden.

Spring is the time to begin planning your herb garden. The prudent gardener will carefully consider the many advantages and benefits of herb planting. By preparing now, you can also assure a good holiday stock of the spicy gifts to brighten up holiday meals.

Fresh or carefully dried herbs from the home garden bear little resemblance to their often pale, lifeless supermarket counterparts. Even if your garden plot is not more than ten feet (three meters) square, there is always room for a few herb plants that can be snipped fresh in summer and then dried.

We tend to associate three herbs with the winter holidays—rosemary, sage, and thyme. The flavor and scent that these plants impart to food are attributable to aromatic essential oils produced by glands present in the leaves and stems.

Rosemary, sage, and thyme have long been known as medicinal and culinary herbs. Their uses are diverse. They can be snipped fresh into soups, sauces, dressings, and a variety of other foods. They can be used to enliven salads and breads, and to make such kitchen staples as herbed vinegar and herbed butter. In substituting fresh herbs for dried herbs, a good rule of thumb seems to be to increase the measure three or four times: three or four parts snipped, loosely packed herbs for each part dried, as specified in the recipe at hand. If possible, as in the case of soups and stews, add the herbs only during the last half of cooking time, since steam tends to demolish their important aromatic essential oils. On the same theory, dried herbs should be stored in a cool, dry cabinet away from daylight and the steam of cooking.

It's great to have a showy spice rack, but if it's hung above the stove, the seasonings may suffer. Even under ideal storage conditions, herbs will only retain their impact so long, and thus the secret is in regular use so as not to let them become too old.

Rosemary, sage, and thyme are all perennials; to keep your kitchen supplied with these herbs throughout the year, you might consider potting a few plants for the kitchen windowsill in the fall. The addition of just a few home grown herbs in pots will add fragrant goodwill to the kitchen of any gardener.

Drying your herb yield is easy

In addition to the quaint mixtures of color and textures you enjoy in your garden, your yield can supply your spice shelf. Drying your spices brings not only a feeling of satisfaction but also a saving, when you consider the inflated prices on the supermarket shelves.

Only modest talent is required to dry herbs from your garden for winter use. Cut the plants in the morning and wash in cool water to remove dust and soil. Tie the stems together in small bunches and hang them in a warm, dry room (an attic is ideal) where they will not be bleached by the sun. After two or three weeks, the leaves should be crackly dry and can be stripped from the stems. The leaves can either be crumbled or left whole until they are used. Do not powder the leaves, since this results in loss of pungency. The ideal storage containers are dark-tinted glass jars or small metal cannisters, but any glass or metal container with a tight-fitting lid can be used. Instead of hanging the herbs to dry, they can be spread in single layers on drying screens. An old window screen will do fine.

Another approach to drying is to cut the leaves and stems into smaller pieces and spread them on a cookie sheet, which can be set on top of the fridge where the fridge warmth will provide the drying. Or, if you're stuck, place it in the oven for a short time at medium heat.

Rosemary, sage, and thyme can be grown in relatively poor but otherwise well-drained and properly limed soils. If the plants are trimmed from time to time, it will only make them grow thicker and bushier. Give them plenty of sunlight.

Rosemary also repels the cabbage moth, bean beetle, and carrot fly, while sage has a similar effect on these bothersome vegetable garden pests, and thyme takes care of the cabbage worm, so they're good companion plants near these vegetables.

There are many herbs available. I suggest you try more than only those I've discussed here.

If you grow your own herbs, perhaps nothing could be more convenient than a ready-made mixture of the appropriate season-

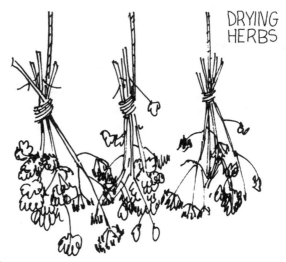

DRYING
HERBS

HANGING

SCREEN

TRAY

ings for poultry dressing. A small amount of this seasoning can also be mixed with butter and used for basting the holiday fowl. In addition this herbal mixture can be mixed with grated cheddar cheese and a few tablespoons of butter, cream, and sherry and then melted over boiling water and cooled to make a delightful herbed cheese; a good proportion is 2 tablespoons (4 ml) seasoning to ½ pound (about ¼ kilogram) of cheese.

Poultry seasoning

(*All measures are for dried herbs*)

2 cups (500 ml) sage, crumbled
½ cup (125 ml) rosemary, ground
¼ cup (60 ml) thyme, crumbled
¼ cup (60 ml) marjoram, crumbled
2 tablespoons (40 ml) salt
1 teaspoon (5 ml) ginger, ground
1 teaspoon (5 ml) pepper, ground.

Combine all ingredients and store in a tightly covered container in a cool, dark place. Small packets of this seasoning make welcome gifts for fellow cooks who lack herb gardens.

Another very aromatic plant that will thrive either in an area within your garden or at the end of a border is spearmint. It has a delightful scent, but do take care that you watch the spreading. It will virtually take over unless kept in check. Many of my gardener friends put their spearmint to good use with new potatoes. A leaf or two thrown in a pot of boiling (or steaming) new potatoes will add a delightful flavor.

Perennials, your permanent show year after year

The time for planting your annuals has arrived, though, of course, we can do this until the end of May. Container grown annuals can be planted throughout the summer.

There is nothing like annuals to give a mass of color to your garden, but I must confess that I have found more joy in perennials, and I now have these spotted throughout my flowerbeds to give a permanent show year after year. It also means I've considerably reduced the amount of annual planting required.

Perennials are flowering, seed bearing, leafy plants whose roots live from year to year. Their tops may or may not die back in winter.

Perennials give color to the garden in shady spots or hot sunny spots. They are excellent in front of shrubs. They are colorful in spring, summer, or fall, even in winter, depending on variety. Most perennials flower the first year.

Usually, perennials will not flower unless they develop to a certain size and are then exposed to low temperatures for a number of weeks and finally exposed to increasing day lengths and increasing temperatures. Their flowering time is the result of this sequence of day length and temperature.

Perennials require a measure of normal care, and they do well in most parts of Canada and the United States. To grow perennials, follow these guidelines.

Prepare the soil in the flowerbeds thoroughly.

Start with vigorous plants or seeds. The best plan is to buy started plants.

Set plants out in spring or fall.

Provide the recommended distances.

Keep some distance between the perennials and the annuals.

Let the perennials stand out. Give them a background to show them off. Evergreens or wooden fences make good backgrounds.

Do not consider leaving the perennials without splitting when they grow big. Splitting gives them and new plants more room to grow.

Provide good drainage and adequate water during summer.

When planting, incorporate manure into the soil. This will help lighten the soil and provide plenty of nutrients.

A 5-15-10 grade fertilizer used at the rate of 1½ pounds (0.7 kilograms) per 100 square feet (10 square meters) should provide the nutrients required for healthy growth.

Select your perennials to suit your needs: edges for walks or pathways, accents in an evergreen planting, a mass effect, a screen of color. You can also select according to the best flowering time, and this may vary from very early spring to summer, fall and, yes, even the middle of winter.

Plan your perennial garden. If you are putting in a full border of perennials, make your border one-third wider than your tallest perennial. Try grouping your show of color. Remember again that you can also put perennials in what is otherwise your annual border or bed to give a greater degree of permanency and reduce the need for annual planting.

Perennials save time and money

I'll only have told half the story about perennials if I fail to point out that there are specific perennials for backdrop duty in your garden and perennials best suited for shady areas.

Not only are background perennials ideal in permanent plantings of perennials, but they're also a super way of reducing the need for expensive and time-consuming annual planting. But perhaps best of all, you'll take care of those more difficult areas against the fence or shrubs.

Perennials for Borders

Carnations — 18 inches (45 centimeters); assorted colors; July to September.

Chinese lantern —2 feet (60 centimeters); red; fall.

Coreopsis — 2 feet (60 centimeters); yellow; all summer.

German iris — 2 feet (60 centimeters); assorted colors; May to July.

Hardy pink — 15 inches (40 centimeters); assorted colors; July to September.

Japanese iris — 2 feet (60 centimeters); assorted colors; June to August.

Liatris — 30 inches (75 centimeters); white or purple; July to September.

Michaelmas daisy — 18 inches (45 centimeters); assorted colors; May to October.

Oriental poppy — 2 to 3 feet (60 to 90 centimeters); red and orange or pink; May to July.

Painted daisy — 2 feet (60 centimeters); assorted colors; May to July.

Red hot poker — 3 feet (90 centimeters); orange and yellow; July to September.

Shasta daisy — 2 feet (60 centimeters); white; all summer.

Stonecrop — 6 inches (15 centimeters); mostly red; July to September.

Sweet William — dwarf 6 inches (15 centimeters); regular 18 inches (45 centimeters); assorted colors; June to August.

Perennials for rockery

Alyssum — 8 inches (20 centimeters); yellow; April to May.

Arabis — 8 inches (20 centimeters); white; April to May.

Aubretia — 6 inches (15 centimeters); purple and blue; April to June.

Coral bells — 12 inches (30 centimeters); deep pink; all summer.

Creeping phlox — 4 inches (10 centimeters); assorted colors; April to June.

Cushion pink — 8 inches (20 centimeters); assorted colors; May to June.

Forget-me-not — 6 inches (15 centimeters); blue; May to June.

Primula and Primrose — assorted colors; February to July.

Rock aster — 8 inches (20 centimeters); blue; May to June.

Sedum acre — 4 inches (10 centimeters); yellow; May to July.

Stonecrop — 6 inches (15 centimeters); red; July to September.

Sedum stolonifera — 6 inches (15 centimeters); brilliant pink; June to August.

Sweet lavender —10 inches (25 centimeters); blue; June to August.

Thrift — 10 inches (25 centimeters); pink; June to July.

Violet — 4 inches (10 centimeters); clear blue; May to June.

Backdrop perennials

Baby's breath — 2½ feet (75 centimeters); white and pink; July to September.

Balloon flower —2 feet (60 centimeters); blue, pink, and white; July to September.

Bleeding heart — 2½ feet (75 centimeters); red and pink; April to May.

Carnation — 18 inches (45 centimeters); assorted colors; June to August.

Chinese lantern —2 feet (60 centimeters); orange; September to October.

Columbine — 2 feet (60 centimeters); assorted colors; May to July.

Coreopsis — 2 feet (60 centimeters); yellow; July to September.

Delphinium — 4 to 5 feet (1 to 1.5 meters); assorted colors; all summer.

Foxglove — 3 feet (90 centimeters); assorted colors; July to August.

German iris — 2½ feet (75 centimeters); assorted colors; May to June.

Gaillardia — 2 feet (60 centimeters); assorted colors; all summer.

Garden marguerite (Anthemis) — 2½ feet (75 centimeters); yellow, gold; all summer.

Hardy mum — 2 to 4 feet (60 centimeters to 1 meter); assorted colors; August to November.

Hollyhock — 5 to 6 feet (1.5 to 2 meters); assorted colors; July to August.

Monarda — 3 feet (90 centimeters); assorted colors; June to August.

Oriental poppy — 3 feet (90 centimeters); assorted colors; May to July.

Painted daisy — 2 feet (60 centimeters); assorted colors; May to July.

Peony — 2 feet (60 centimeters); assorted colors; May to June.

Perennial sweet pea — Climbing; assorted colors; June to August.

Phlos — 3 feet (90 centimeters); assorted colors; June to September.

Red hot poker — 3 feet (90 centimeters); orange and yellow; July to September.

Shasta daisy — 2 feet (60 centimeters); white; all summer.

Tall michaelmas daisy —4 to 5 feet (1.5 meters); assorted colors; August to October.

Perennials for shade

Ajuga — Groundcover, 8 inches (20 centimeters); blue, May to July.

Forget-me-not — 8 to 12 inches (20 to 30 centimeters); white, pink, and blue; April to October.

Jacob's ladder — 12 inches (30 centimeters); blue; May to July.

Lily of the valley — Groundcover, 8 inches (20 centimeters); white; May to June.

Lungwort (Pulmonaria)—12 inches (30 centimeters); blue and pink; April to June.

Monkshood — 4 to 5 feet (1 to 1.5 meters); blue; July to September.

Oenothera (Sun drops) —2 feet (60 centimeters); yellow; May to September.

Plantain lily — 3 feet (90 centimeters); white and blue; July to August.

Primrose — 8 to 12 inches (20 to 30 centimeters); assorted colors; March to May.

Trollius — 18 inches (45 centimeters); orange and yellow; April to July.

Bill helps a gardener friend, Senator Ray Perrault, select some favorite plants.

Shasta daisies, delphiniums, phlox, and lupines all make
excellent background perennials.

Plant your annuals now

There are more than 1,000 varieties of annuals, although normally only the most popular varieties are marketed as plants, and seeds are sold for the more unusual or exclusive strains.

Annuals bloom quickly and profusely very shortly after planting, and the plants grow fairly large in a relatively short time. Annuals should be planted wherever possible in fairly large groupings to get the most impressive show. One large mass of petunias or begonias will get more comments from neighbors than a number of small clumps spotted around the yard. In deciding where to plant annuals, pick an area where you want attention drawn or where beauty and color can be added.

In caring for annuals, select plants that are best suited to the location. Most annuals like a sunny spot, but some, such as coleus, impatiens, and begonias, prefer shade. As with all flowers, provide a backdrop for your plantings. This may be a fence, hedge, foundation, evergreen, flowering tree or a bed of tall perennials.

Water the plants well, but don't drown them. Annuals don't look their best during a rainy season since water drops on the flowers and they may close up, thus encouraging disease.

When watering, try to get the water as much as possible on the soil rather than the flowers. Watering in early morning is best, and watering at night is worst.

To keep annuals healthy, remove dead blooms. Cut the blooms you want for that vase indoors and remove the others when they're dry.

Cut petunias back when they get scraggly.

If plants have begun flowering when purchased, pinch the buds and blooms off during planting. This will produce more blooms and at a much faster rate.

When planting, be sure not to disturb the roots any more than necessary. Plant sufficiently deep but not too deep. Water well after planting, and within a few days, water with a liquid fertilizer such as fish or Hi-Sol (20-20-20), mixing two level tablespoons (4 ml) per gallon (4 liters) of water to stimulate root growth. Always firm the plants in when planting.

I've provided more about annuals in the May chapter so you won't forget the basics at planting time.

Roses, roses, roses—the garden ruler

Without doubt, roses are still the most popular flowering bush in the garden.

They provide a continuous showing of glorious color all summer and fall. Roses are available in many forms: dwarf bushes for borders and beds; taller bushes for large, individual blooms; very tall bushes for screens or hedges; ramblers and climbers to cover fences or walls; and tree roses to provide a focal point along the driveway or in the middle of a rose garden.

There are numerous opportunities for the best use and maximum beauty from your rose bushes, but one should really understand the basic differences between the various types to ensure the best possible results.

> ***Hybrid tea roses*** Large buds and blooms, long stems, and a lasting period of bloom have made hybrid teas the most widely known flowers in the world. Enjoy them along walks, with evergreens, in foundation plantings, or in flower beds.
>
> ***Floribundas*** Very floriferous, producing many clusters of from fifteen to twenty-five blooms. They flower continuously from June until the first frost. They are excellent around foundations or in borders and along walkways and driveways. More about Floribundas later in this chapter.
>
> ***Grandifloras*** Each branch holds a bouquet—a cluster of large blooms on tall stems. The bush grows taller than its parents, the floribunda and hybrid tea, and can be used for cutting to make a fragrant, long-lasting flower arrangement.
>
> The grandiflora bushes are excellent for background plantings, for hedges or screens, or to use on the sunny side of the house for foundation planting.

Climbing roses   Climbers are vigorous and easy to grow. Train them against a trellis, pole, rose arbor, fence, or bare wall. Climbing roses do not always bloom the first year; a number of varieties bloom only on second-year wood.

Tree roses   These are garden highlights. They are like a bush on a tall stem and bloom every bit as profusely. Tree roses are also excellent in containers on balconies or patios.

When planting roses, bareroot or from a package, dig the hole deep and wide enough to allow the roots to be spread in a natural position.

The soil you have removed from the hole should be mixed with manure or peat moss. Use one part of this organic material to two parts of your soil. The organic material will add needed nutrients and also allow the soil to hold moisture, while permitting proper drainage.

Adding the peat moss or manure is very important if your soil is sand or heavy clay. When planting in containers, also use a mixture of one part manure and two parts good soil.

Trim off any roots or stems that have been broken. Build a mound of soil in the hole to support the roots and hold the plant high enough so that the bud union is at ground level. Fill the hole two-thirds full of soil mixture, and firm down lightly with your feet to remove any air pockets. Fill the rest of the hole with water and let it soak in. Then fill the hole with soil mixture and firm gently.

When planting container-grown rosebushes, dig the hole slightly deeper and wider than the depth and diameter of the container. Fill the bottom of the hole with the same soil mix described earlier. Remove the rosebush from the pot, being careful not to disturb the soil ball and set in the hole so that the bud union is at ground level. Fill the soil mix around the bush, firm, and water well. More about roses in containers a bit later.

Container roses must be fed regularly with a good rose food.

Give roses plenty of room

Roses should not be planted too near a wall, as this would cause them to grow leggy and forward. Bushes must be planted 18 to 24 inches (45 to 60 centimeters) away from buildings or fences.

Roses must have air circulating all around them. If they are planted where there is a lack of circulating air, they are prone to powdery mildew and blackspot.

Don't plant roses too close to other bushes, trees, or shrubs, as these tap the water and food supply. Roses should get four to six hours of sunshine daily.

Plant your hybrid tea roses about 30 inches (75 centimeters) apart; your floribunda roses 24 inches (60 centimeters) apart and your grandiflora 27 inches (70 centimeters) apart. Climbing roses that you wish to train along a solid wall should be planted 12 to 15 inches (30 to 38 centimeters) away from the wall, as the soil near the building is usually shallow.

However, for climbers against a fence, arbor, or trellis, the planting may be closer.

Climbing roses should be spaced 4 feet (1 meter) apart. Tree roses need to be 4 feet (1 meter) from each other. When planting bush roses around a tree rose, follow the distances set forth above, depending on type.

Bill and Lillian display a container grown rosebush.

When growing roses in containers on the patio or balcony, make sure the container is at least 12 inches (30 centimeters) in diameter and 12 to 14 inches (30 to 35 centimeters) deep. Make certain the container has ample drainage; it is preferable to place small cleats under the container and a light layer of gravel in the bottom.

Plant the rosebush or tree so that the bud union is 1 to 2 inches (2.5 to 5 centimeters) beneath the top of the soil and the top of the soil 2 inches (5 centimeters) below the top ridge of the container.

Leaving a space above the soil in the container allows for a convenient water reservoir and avoids splashing when watering. The top part may be covered with plain or ornamental gravel for looks and to help keep the moisture in and the slugs out.

During the growing season, soil in containers must be kept moist. If you can feel no moisture 1 inch (2.5 centimeters) below the surface, the plant needs more water.

After the new growth is about 8 inches (20 centimeters) long, fertilize weekly with liquid fertilizer. Use half the recommended amount until the plant is growing well, and then increase to the amount recommended on the package.

Dilute with enough water to distribute the mixture evenly throughout the entire container.

Roses in containers can stand winter temperatures down to 28°F (-2°C) without any covering or protection but if the temperature drops below this, you should bury the container and partially cover the bush with straw, sawdust, or leafmold or move it into a protected, covered area. Do not water except to keep from going completely dry, and do not move into an area where they would sprout prematurely.

Queen of flowers in every size and color

The rose has been on earth for many millions of years, but it was not until the last 80 years or so that the rose gained full recognition. Thanks to the great work of many wonderful plant breeders, we now have a full array of types, sizes, and colors, and all are direct descendants of the old-fashioned shrub rose.

Golden slippers, a popular floribunda rose.

The old-fashioned shrub rose is still sought after, perhaps mostly by those who have moved to the Northwest from the Prairie provinces or midwestern regions of the United States and who would like a plant or two just for sentimental reasons. The old shrub roses grow tall and bushy, and they are generally quite thorny—but oh, that fragrance! Somehow they help us remember the old times. I can well remember the old rugosa single pink rose growing along the railroad track. I used to walk along that track to school, and as kids we loved them and picked them just for a small fragrant bouquet.

The old shrub roses are still grown today. The wild rugosa variety that is so well known to all of us, but in particular to Albertans, who claim it as their provincial emblem, is generally used as an understock for budding or grafting tree roses. The shrub roses have also been improved over the centuries. The *Rosa gallica*, red rose of Lancaster, was cultivated by the ancient Greeks. *Rosa alba*, white rose of York, was brought to England by the Romans. The newer rugosa types are in many ways superior, however, especially since they are repeat flowers as opposed to the once only blooming varieties. The old-fashioned moss roses, known for their outstanding fragrance, are also the result of more recent breeding, but they are often hard to get, and one should actually order these by color from the nursery a year in advance. Strangely enough, an old-fashioned rose will now cost you about double the price of a regular rose, as they are not mass-produced but are selectively grown by a few and persistent oldtimers.

It was only about one hundred years ago when a French hybridizer raised the first hybrid tea rose. The rose was appropriately named La France. The hybrid tea came from the hybrid perpetual parentage that was popular during the nineteenth century. The name "tea rose" came from the fact that those initial discoveries had a tealike scent, which, unfortunately, has been lost over the years and now actually is quite rare. The hybrid tea

Tropicana, a favorite hybrid tea rose.

rose has, of course, been perfected in quality of both bloom and color. As a matter of fact, it was quite some time before the first yellow rose, Soleil d'Or, was discovered, and from this, hundreds of hues, color combinations, and unusual shades evolved.

For a time we lost the lovely rose scents

It is truly unfortunate that the fragrance of roses was lost in the hybridizing process, and it has been only recently that newer varieties have become available which recapture some of the delightful fragrance. Rose fanciers demanded it, the hybridizers went to work, and varieties like tropicana have proven that it can be done. Tropicana, incidentally, is a warm, orange-colored rose, which has a distinct raspberry fragrance. Hybrid tea roses are borne singly or in small groups and are generally of good size, making them most popular for formal rose beds, cutting, and exhibiting. The hybrid tea rose is by far the most popular and outsells all other roses three to one. There are literally hundreds of varieties available, but let me name just a few of my favorites.

Peace rose This has been the world's best seller. It has huge blooms that are very durable, pale yellow, edged with pink. The Chicago peace has much deeper color than the original, but otherwise they are very similar. Pink peace is even bigger and enjoys a superior fragrance to its counterparts in the peace group.

Pascali This is my favorite white. It has medium-sized blooms, is fairly disease resistant, and has some fragrance.

Royal Highness This is the rose with the exquisite form. It is almost perfect, and it offers a delicious perfume. The rose is like a painting, displaying all shades of pastel pink.

King's ransom, gold crown, and summer sunshine In the yellows I favor these varieties.

Fragrant cloud I have already mentioned tropicana, but fragrant cloud rivals it in both color and quality. It is a beautiful rose with a strong and delightful perfume.

Wendy Cussons, Ena Harkness, Chrysler imperial, and Papa Meilland These are my favorite reds. Each of these varieties displays extra large blooms, are double, and have rich fragrance.

There are also some very unusual colors in the hybrid tea group. The following examples are only a few of the many unusual hybrid teas available these days. Of the unusual types, these are some of the easiest to grow.

Blue moon — A large double, fragrant blue.

Sterling silver — A lovely lilac shade.

Rose gaujard — An unusual color combination of red and white.

Granada — An outstanding two-tone of red and gold.

For those of you who enjoy cutting your roses to display in your favorite places indoors, your best purchases by far would be peace, tropicana, sterling silver, Miss Ireland, granada, and fragrant cloud.

Rose bushes can be purchased bareroot in late fall or early spring, packaged in mid-spring season, or potted in late spring and throughout the summer. The advantage to purchasing a potted rose is that you can actually see the type of foliage and perhaps even the shape, size, and color of the blooms.

Hybrid tea roses are available as bush-types, half-standard tree, or full-standard tree, and also in climbing form.

Remember that roses require plenty of sun, but slight shade during early afternoon is beneficial. Roses also need plenty of air. They just don't do well shut in by other plants or walls. Plenty of air helps keep them free of diseases. Roses simply do not grow well under trees. They should be planted in medium loam that is slightly acid and reasonably rich in plant food and humus.

Proper rose care extends plant life span

Once you've planted your rose bushes, you must remember your job is only half done. The after-planting care is as important as your variety selection and soil preparation.

There are numerous good rose sprays and dusts. Many are excellent, and different rosegrowers have their own preferences. My favorite spray or paint-on insecticide is Lagon or Cygon. These two are systemic insecticides, meaning that they are absorbed through the veins of the leaves, and therefore have long-lasting results. In addition, they also prevent the killing of the helpful bug eaters like the ladybug.

I use it about once a month, starting soon after the first good crop of leaves appears. I prefer to use it in the early morning before the weather warms.

My first choice as a fungicide is Benomyl or Funginex. Again, these are systemic, and thus, unlike the old-fashioned sprays, they do not wash off. They are absorbed directly into the bush, giving lasting protection.

If either of these are used at about two week intervals, you'll keep clean bushes, climbers, and trees, and avoid the disastrous effects of blackspot, mildew, or rust. I always add some fish fertilizer or a few drops of "spreader sticker" to the mix, which not only provides a more thorough coverage all over the bush but also allows the material to stick properly, thereby making it more effective and preventing the loss of valuable spray run-off.

If you suspect any disease or see evidence of attacking insects, take a diseased portion to your favorite nursery where it can be identified and treatment prescribed.

After my roses are in full leaf I begin to apply a rose food. Often, if roses lack the proper nutrients such as nitrogen, phosphate, or potash, and, almost as important, the best balance of other necessary elements such as magnesium, boron, and zinc, the leaves will discolor, spot, or develop sickly-looking edges, all of which give the appearance of disease, when in fact it is a deficiency.

I prefer a dry rose food, of which I spread 2 heaping

tablespoons (4 ml) around the base of the bush and scratch it in, following immediately with a good watering. I feed when the plants are in full leaf, again after the first bloom, and again in mid-August.

Never fertilize after the middle of September, as this would create soft growth prior to winter frosts subject to freezing.

Always plant the roses where there is ample drainage. Roses do not like wet feet, yet they must not be allowed to dry out. Check the soil often with your heel or a tool, and if the soil is dry 1 or 2 inches (2.5 to 5 centimeters) below the surface, you'll need to give them a good watering.

A trickle of ground watering is preferred, and you'll need to water sufficiently to soak the soil to a 6-inch (15-centimeter) depth. If you find you must water the roses over top, make sure there's the opportunity for the foliage to dry before nightfall. Do not water your roses in the evening, for if they go to bed with wet foliage, they are the perfect target for rose diseases.

Cultivate regularly around your roses but do so shallowly, so as not to injure any roots growing near the surface. Cultivating helps keep the moisture in and the weeds out.

If you spread a 2-inch (5-centimeter)layer of barkmulch or peatmoss around the bushes, you'll not need to cultivate, as this accomplishes the same result.

If you are primarily interested in fewer but larger exhibition-type blooms (maybe you'll want to compete in the local rose show or country fair) you'll have to disbud. This involves pinching out the side buds with your fingers while the buds are still very small, leaving only the top flower on each stem.

Transplanting and pruning

If you're thinking about transplanting rosebushes, do so in the late fall, when they are completely dormant. Very early spring is okay too.

Prune the bush back to about 18 to 24 inches (45 to 60 centimeters) for ease of handling. Whenever possible, dig the bush with a ball of earth (this is easier if you soak the soil thoroughly the night before). Replant immediately and tramp the soil down firmly followed with another good watering.

It is too late for spring pruning this year, but perhaps the following bit of information will make for a better crop next year.

The best time to prune is in the early spring before growth starts, sometime after the last real killing frost. It is not advisable to prune after the new growth is 2 or 3 inches (5 or 7 centimeters) long.

Always make an angle cut with a good sharp rose pruner. Make the cut ¼ inch (0.6 centimeters) above an outside bud eye, slanting downward toward the inside of the bush at a 45-degree angle.

In general prune back by about a third, leaving two-thirds of the bush to grow; some prefer to cut back shorter and if regularly pruned, they can be cut back to as low as 8 inches (20 centimeters) above the bud union (climbers are the exception). Prune out the center of the bush for air circulation. Weak or diseased canes should be removed completely.

Any branch that crosses or rubs against another should also be removed. Cut back any winter-killed branches to about 2 inches (5 centimeters) below the winter-killed portion—cut just above the nearest live leafbud (a reddish swelling in the bark of the cane).

Climbing roses often bloom on only the second year or older wood and thus should be thinned out by only about ten percent per year. Cut out any diseased canes or old, nonproductive canes.

I do summer pruning as well. This means that I cut off all the spent blooms to encourage new summer growth for more bloom. I usually cut back to about several buds below the bloom head and prune, as normal, on a slant.

Come late fall, after the first real hard frost, I remove all the leaves and rake up everything around the bushes.

If old leaves are left, they'll possibly lead to disease the next year. I prune back the big tops just a little to give a cleaner-looking effect and spray with dormant oil and lime sulphur for the first cleaning.

I cover the bud unions with a mound of earth of about 4 to 6 inches (10 to 15 centimeters) to provide some added winter protection in case of severe cold.

It's hard to beat the floribunda rose

My favorite roses are the floribundas, because they are extremely floriferous and dwarf in growth habits. Floribunda roses are available in bush, climbing, and tree form. The blooms come in large trusses or clusters and cover the bush from early summer often until Christmas. The floribunda roses are great in flower beds where you want a mass showing, but they are also excellent along driveways or walkways, providing a continuous riot of color. For my money, it is hard to beat the floribunda rose.

The person most responsible for the development and improvement of this increasingly popular group of roses is a Mr. Poulsen of Denmark. Mr. Poulsen crossed a hybrid tea rose with the hybrid polyantha and so created the floribunda in the year 1924. After much further development, thanks to such people as Harry Wheatcroft of Britain, another important category of rose, the grandiflora rose, was developed.

The grandiflora rose bears its flowers in clusters like the floribunda, but the blooms are about the size of a hybrid tea, and the bush grows much taller than its parents, sometimes to a height of 6 feet (2 meters). The most famous of the grandiflora roses is Queen Elizabeth, a lovely shaped bush with pink blooms.

I should list some of my favorite floribunda roses, but first of all I must tell you about my all-time favorite floribunda rose called Europeana. This unbelievable beauty just seems to bloom forever, but even before the display of blooms, its foliage alone is a picture. The Europeana rose has a shining bronze and green foliage and very early breaks into huge, long-lasting clusters of brilliant shades of red, though predominantly blood red (or, as some call it, Spanish red). The bush is more disease resistant than most, and because of its extremely healthy growth, it even appears to withstand the bugs better than its brothers.

Sarabanda Another of my favorites, a dwarf compact bush with dazzling orange-red single blooms with yellow stamens to crown its beauty.

All gold A compact bush with glossy foliage and nonfading yellow blooms.

Iceberg A tremendously prolific white, although taller than most.

Circus A blend of gold, orange, and red.

Masquerade Yellow, red, and orange blooms, all on one bush.

Little darling The most delicate shade of pink.

Lavender girl A deep shade of lavender.

Elizabeth of Glamis A deep salmon, famous for its fragrance.

Remember this about our floribunda roses: they have a longer flowering season and bloom more continuously than the hybrid teas. They are much superior in bloom during wet summers than other types. The floribunda rose is hardier and will generally withstand severe frosts. They are easier to grow, especially in the more sandy soils where others would fail. They are more colorful, providing intense splashes of color.

Miniature roses

The Spanish have done some of the finest work in hybridizing the miniature rose. Spaniards with relatively small gardens and a usually short supply of water set out to develop roses they could grow in pots, window boxes, and rockeries.

When grown in confined areas, miniature roses do need frequent water and feeding, but otherwise, although small in size of bush and bloom, they resemble the regular rose in every detail. Several of my favorite varieties follow.

Little buckaroo A good double bright red.

Baby masquerade A compact bush only 8 inches

tall, and all colors of bloom are produced on one bush.

Coralin   A double coral red and scarlet gem, the brightest red of all.

Climbing roses

Finally, there is the climbing rose, and there are two main types: the ramblers, and the more modern floribunda and hybrid tea climbers.

The ramblers are suitable for covering arches, gazebos, and screens, but not walls, as some are prone to mildew. They can bring a mass of color during summer, but there is generally only a single flush of color, and the blooms are small. Some of the best known varieties are Dorothy Perkins, zepherin, exelsa, albertine, and new dawn.

The floribunda and hybrid tea climbers are repeat flowering and bear large blooms. Remember that these types produce many more blooms if the side growths are trained horizontally and not vertically. Don't expect too much from climbers during the first year; they do take some time to become properly established.

Roses, like most other garden plants, make heavy demands on the reserves of plant foods in the soil. If one or more of the vital nutrients or elements are missing, then hunger signs appear on the leaves or flowers or both. The recognizable signs are premature petal fall, poor disease resistance, a plant that is particularly attractive to bugs, pale or discolored leaves, and stunted growth or weak stems. You may foliar feed (feeding the foliage by spraying) or use a powder-type compound fertilizer. Remember, once again, weak, underfed roses are most prone to bugs and disease, so feed well.

Established roses have deep roots and will not require much watering. You will need to water plenty during a dry spell, especially in sandy soils. A bush rose usually requires about a gallon (4 liters) of water, and a climber up to 3 gallons (12 liters) a day.

To keep roses blooming profusely during the entire summer and into fall, you will need to summer prune or "dead head".

This is the regular removal of dead blooms. With established floribundas, the whole truss should be removed, and shoots bearing dead hybrid tea blooms should be removed to about half their length. The cut should be made ¼ inch (0.6 centimeters) above a leaf and outward-facing bud.

April wrap-up on shrubs

Perhaps the most popular shrubs are the rhododendrons and azaleas. The Japanese evergreen dwarf azaleas, which come in a spectrum of colors—red, pink, purple, and white—are now becoming a must in everyone's garden.

Of course, they are extremely colorful at this time of the year, but they are also very hardy, and they do well both in the sun and in areas of partial shade. The fact that they are low-growing evergreens and relatively care-free makes them a good choice for rockery, border, and planters.

The rhododendrons fare extremely well, also. However, many gardeners still fail to realize that rhododendrons, like azaleas and camellias, are surface-rooted shrubs, and if they are forced to compete with nearby grass, trees or other shrubs, they are soon robbed of every nutrient required, and they quickly begin to yellow and look anemic, failing to produce the expected bloom.

I can't stress strongly enough the need to use an acid-type fertilizer, containing not only nitrogen, phosphorous and potash, but also the important element iron. I remind many customers that those pesky weevils—¼ inch (0.6 centimeters) long, black, and beetlelike—chew at the rhododendron leaves at night and attack the roots during the day.

The solution, of course, is to put out weevil bait at the base of the plant. The weevils will then pick up the bait and carry it back to their colonies where, we hope, the evening feast will wipe out the lot. Another solution is to spray thoroughly with Malathion.

Evergreens, especially for hedges or screens, are always much in demand, but contrary to the trend when I was active in the nursery trade, the demand has gone from an inexpensive little shrub to "what's the biggest and best you can find for me?"

103

Fortunately, the majority of gardeners have learned about the dreaded cypress root rot (possibly they've learned the hard way), and the demand now is for cedars. Nine out of ten evergreens now sold either are junipers or cedars, with the cypress (which was once the most popular shrub) a distant third.

Remember fruit trees for beauty and bounty

It's amazing how many people are planting fruit trees. Perhaps the increased prices of fruit have something to do with this trend. Fruit trees of every description are in great demand. The fact that they now come ready-pruned and container-planted has helped sales a hundredfold. By all means ask your nursery for advice.

Q: My lettuce seeds are germinating very poorly and slowly. What is the cause?
A: You are probably keeping the seeds too warm.

Q: Can I plant the old "mum" plants I got at Easter outdoors?
A: Yes, plant them after blooming. Feed well and the plant will bloom again in the garden in fall.

Q: Many years ago my mother told me about an herb that was beneficial in treating rheumatism. Can you tell me the name of it?
A: The herb is called borage. The leaves can be preserved in vinegar. They will smell and taste like cucumber. They can also be eaten like spinach.

Q: Why have I mildew on my roses in April and what can I do about it?
A: The dark weather and lack of a breeze probably are the causes. The best remedy is Benomyl, with a little liquid fish fertilizer to help it adhere to the leaves.

Q: My evergreens look anemic and tend to grow brown inside every year.
A: They probably are anemic and starved. Try feeding with a good evergreen fertilizer and keep well watered in summer and fall.

Q: How do I keep from losing my sprays through run-off?
A: Good question! Add three tablespoons of liquid fish fertilizer to every gallon (4 liters) of spray mix. It acts as a sticker.

Q: I like growing tomatoes in my little greenhouse. Can you recommend a variety?
A: Try Alsa Craig.

Q: Is there really such a thing as a tree tomato?
A: Yes. It's a tomatillo. The tree grows to 12 feet (4 meters) but can be trimmed. The leaves are huge and it takes 3 years to bear. The fruit is delicious.

Q: Is there a safe fungicide I can use to prevent gray mold, tomatoleaf mold, and other blights or mildew?
A: The best is Benomyl, used fairly regularly.

Q: I lose many seedlings to cutworms, especially my cabbage and lettuce. What can I do?
A: When planting, sprinkle Diazinon granules into the soil and if you still have trouble, scratch (cultivate) regularly around the plants when small and you'll probably pick out the cutworms from the soil.

Q: I can't grow grass in the shady area behind my home.
A: Yes you can. Try a shade-loving grass called *Poa trivialis.*

Q: My salvia are all chewed off. What is it?
A: Try slug bait in either pellet, bran, or liquid form. I prefer the bran type, and sprinkle it lightly once every 10 days all along the edges of the flowerbeds.

Q: Do I have to do anything to my tulips and daffodils after flowering?

A: After the bulbs have bloomed to their fullest, cut or pull off the flowerheads, leaving the stem. Allow the foliage to die down naturally. The foliage in its dying days returns the nutrients from stem and leaves to the bulbs where they're stored for the next year.

Q: Do I have to dig up my bulbs each year?

A: I have left my crocus, hyacinths, tulips, and daffodils for the third year without digging and they're still blooming beautifully. My snowdrops and grape hyacinths have been in the same spot going on 8 years. I do dig the summer and fall blooming bulbs each October and store them in a cool part of the basement over winter. If you haven't got a basement, any cool area that won't be touched with frost will do.

Q: Can I plant my Easter lilies outside?

A: You bet your boots, and odds are they will bloom again the same time next year and for years to come. The wise gardener will often collect leftover Easter lilies from garden centers and flower shops after the holiday at bargain prices.

Q: When and why should I use weed preventer?

A: After you clear and work up the flowerbeds or when all the soil is hoed and raked between your shrubs or perennials, you can sprinkle on the weed preventer. The preventer will not harm the existing shrubs and plants or affect your bulbs or bedding plants when planted after application, but it does prevent weeds from growing and saves a lot of hoeing and weeding all summer.

May

Outdoor planting too early for some varieties

In late April and early May we tend to be a bit too eager to put in our gardens. But it is still quite cool, especially for some of the more tender plants like annuals.

We often get several warm days and feel confident that it will continue. However, plants put outdoors will suffer setbacks if a cold snap comes. In the warmer climates annuals can be sown directly outdoors, but in our climate the annuals, be they flower or such vegetables as tomatoes, peppers, cucumbers, and most others, excepting beans, peas, radishes, carrots, spinach, and the other quick germinating varieties, must wait until we are sure of warmer nights.

Hold off on planting salvia, ageratum, marigolds, impatiens, and other flowering plants, as well as tomatoes, peppers, cucumbers, and tender vegetables, until daytime temperatures average about 60°F (15°C) and night temperatures fall to no less than 46 to 50°F (8 to 10°C).

Many people purchase their annuals early, while they are still small. They then transplant them into small pots and keep them indoors until they are a large size. This will give them a head start.

The most common mistake with sowing indoors is starting too early. If they are started too early, they will grow up tall, spindly, and yellow, and it will be impossible to put them outside unless you have a cold frame with some heat. You should normally start your bedding plant seeds about five weeks ahead of the last frost, which for the northwest region, would be the middle of March.

I cannot recommend that you depend on home-grown seeds, that is, the ones you carry over from your own plants from the previous year. The problem is that some plants cross-pollinate very readily, such as cucumbers, squashes, beets, turnips, and others. Some plants produce seeds that revert to the original parentage; phlox is a good example of this, and hybrids will not come true from seed again.

Some rules to follow if you start your seeds in containers

Any flat box or other container is suitable. You can also use halved milk or egg cartons. If there are no drainage holes in the container, make some.

Soil, peat moss, vermiculite, sand, and starter mix, which is a ready mix, can be used for growing seeds. You need porosity for good drainage and good water retention capacity, and the mix must be sterilized so that there are no bugs, diseases, or weeds. Add 1 level teaspoon (2 ml) of 5-10-5 (or near equivalent), fertilize, and add 2 level tablespoons (4 ml) of agricultural lime to every 10 pounds (5 kilograms) of soil.

You can also use your garden soil, mixing it with equal parts of peat and washed sand and sterilizing the mix in your oven by preheating it to 180°F (81°C). Place the mix in a shallow pan, making sure it's moist but not wet. Place a 2-inch (5-centimeter) wedge of new potato in the middle of the pan. When the potato is easily pierced with a fork, the soil mix is sterile. Turn off the oven, but leave the pan inside to cool. Again, add fertilizer to this mix by adding 1 tablespoon (2 ml) of superphosphate, 1 tablespoon (2 ml) of agricultural lime, and 1 tablespoon (2 ml) of bonemeal for each 5 pounds (2 kilograms) of mix. When the mix is cool, it's ready to use. If it's not used immediately, store in a sealed plastic bag.

When you are ready to sow seeds, fill clean containers to ½ inch (1 centimeter) from the top. Moisten and allow to stand overnight to allow excess water to drain away. Form the surface gently with your hands. Sow small seeds shallowly, large seeds more deeply, then sow the seeds in rows about 1½ inches (4 centimeters) apart. Sprinkle with a fine water spray. Set the container in sufficient water so that the soil mix will absorb from the bottom until it is all moist. When the soil mix is moist, cover the container with glass or clean plastic. Do not allow soil surface to dry.

Warm temperatures from 70-80°F (20-25°C) are needed to germinate seeds. Drastic temperature fluctuations may kill seeds.

When the seedlings push through the surface, remove the glass or plastic covering. Move the seedlings to good light. Cooler temperatures, such as 70-80°F (20-25°C) during the day and 60°F

(15°C) at night are in order. If seedlings get spindly, you'll need more light.

When seedlings are 1 inch (2.5 centimeters) tall and before true leaves are well developed, it is time to thin them out. Thin seedlings to about 1 inch (2.5 centimeters) apart. Begin feeding weekly with a liquid 5-15-10 fertilizer. Always make sure the growing mix is moist before watering with the fertilizer mix. Do not pour feed on tender plants. Never overwater, or damping off will develop. Roots die from insufficient oxygen, and the stem rots at soil level. If a gray mold develops on top of the soil, you are overwatering.

When this happens, allow the soil mix to dry until the plants begin to wilt, and then poke or break up the soil between the plants with a dinner fork. Use water warmed to room temperature.

When three leaves have formed, you can transplant seedlings to individual pots. When transplanting, hold the plant gently by the leaves, not the stem, so as not to bruise the plant, as this, too, can cause death. Water the transplants and keep them in the shade for the first day.

Two or three weeks before planting in the garden, harden off the young vegetable plants. Flowering plants do not require hardening off.

The best way to harden off is in a cold frame, which is covered at night and opened during the day. The amount of opening depends on daytime temperatures. If you expect a cold night, you may cover the cold frame with a blanket. Without a cold frame, you must carry them in and out.

The old lawn headache, veronica

Every spring I recall being asked at least six times in one day, "What should be used to kill veronica in the lawn?" Veronica is that low, creeping plant that resembles chickweed but bears tiny blue flowers. It spreads like fury all over the lawn and chokes out everything, especially your lawn grass!

That's why it is also frequently referred to as the iron weed. It is particularly tough to kill, and every time you walk over it, you spread it to another part of the lawn. An effective treatment available is a product like MCPA.

MCPA is a liquid herbicide, which works well in combating buttercup, clover, horsetail (marestail), and veronica. You'll need to apply it at the rate of 2 tablespoons (4 ml) per gallon (4 liters) of water, applied with a watering can, over 200 square feet (20 square meters) of lawn area.

The best time to treat the lawn would be on a warm, sunny day, and the treatment should be repeated after two weeks, and again two weeks later. The repeat treatments are required because veronica is a particularly difficult weed to control.

Pests

It never fails to astonish me just how many people honestly believe that plants, whether indoor or outdoor, can thrive simply with the aid of rain or tap water. Plants, like you and me, must eat, and a diet of plain water will eventually weaken them to the point where they are unable to withstand disease or attack by bugs, and they soon die. Plants usually let you know that they are in distress through the discoloration of their foliage or simply by refusing to flower.

Indoor plants, when improperly watered or when their feeding is neglected, often are attacked by red spider mites.

Everyone wonders just where the red spider mites come from, but believe me, they're everywhere, including your home. Given the proper conditions, they soon find their way to your plants. I still find the most effective spray against the red spider mite is 2 tablespoons (4 ml) of Malathion per gallon (4 liters) of water, plus 8 drops of spreader sticker or a tablespoon (2 ml) of dormant oil.

Also, many people at this time of year ask about deep-rooted buttercups and morning glory growing amongst perennials and shrubs in the rockery. You can't spray the rockery, as obviously you would kill the perennials and shrubs as well as the pesky weeds, yet the weeds can't be pulled out because they are too deeply-rooted and too entangled.

Purchase a can of brush killer, which you can paint or dab on the weeds with a small paint brush. The brush killer will translocate through the leaves to the roots and thus rid your garden of that problem.

First week of May is bedding plant time

During May, nearly all flower seeds can be sown in the garden. Fine seeds, like those of the petunia, may be kept in place and from getting too dry by covering them with wet newspaper. Remove the cover as soon as the seeds germinate.

In the flower beds where you want the bulbs of daffodils and tulips to remain for next spring, sow the seeds of annuals between the rows. Annual phlox, California poppies, nasturtiums, and other annuals are good for this purpose.

Garden centers are stocked to the brim with bedding plants, and now is your opportunity to obtain yours from the widest selection and plants of prime quality. Be sure to enrich the soil by mixing in ample well-rotted mushroom manure, which is available by the bag (and it's cheap) at most garden centers, or you can use an all-purpose fertilizer.

Give your sweet peas the support they need now, otherwise they will be too far advanced and tangled, making the job difficult, if not impossible, later on.

Watch your perennials for aphids or lice. Perennial lupines are likely victims, and may require spraying with Malathion.

Prepare your window boxes now by mixing about 1/3 of well-rotted mushroom manure in with the existing soil. Stir it up well. When planting your window boxes, don't skimp on the plant material. Here's a few popular examples of effective planting.

Sun

Annual phlox	Geraniums, ageratum
Dwarf marigolds	Geraniums, upright ice plant
Geraniums, trailing	Nasturtiums
Geraniums, upright	Portulaca

112

Shade

Coleus
Fibrous begonias
Fuchsias, trailing
Fuchsias, upright
Impatiens
Lobelia, trailing
Nepeta
Schizanthus (poor man's orchids)
Tuberous begonia, trailing
Tuberous begonias, upright
Upright begonias and wandering Jew

As summer approaches, keep the faded flowers picked from pansies and voilas to encourage new bloom.

Pinch back plants like the annual chrysanthemums and phlox to make them bush but don't pinch back the nonbranching kinds like lupines.

This year do yourself a big favor and put in a cutting garden bed. Annuals can supply huge quantities of flowers throughout the summer and fall, bringing both color and fragrance indoors to enhance your living day after day. It's cheap because, when you cut properly, the plants will bush again and again, producing more lovelies for your dining room table, kitchen, bedroom, and bathroom.

The cutting garden or bed can be in a secluded area of the garden or a multifunctional border along a driveway or by the vegetables. Prepare the soil deep and well, once more working in manure or substituting all-purpose fertilizer. Keep the bed well watered initially, and feed once more in summer, preferably during an off-time when the food and water will bring on a new burst of growth.

The two qualities a flower should have to recommend it for cutting purposes are long enough stems and a long life. Other than this, grow anything you want.

Experiment with color

Select your colors to match the wallpaper or furnishing or those that will bring a specially beautiful fragrance to a bedside bouquet in the guest room.

Some men don't really appreciate fully the finer things in life and may think it silly that you select the garden pinks to match the painting on your china tea set, until the guests commend your good taste and thoughtfulness.

The cutting garden is an ideal spot for trying out new and unfamiliar varieties. Perhaps you are uncertain about color or growth habit. Grow here the annuals with nonglamorous habits, such as salpiglossis, excellent for bouquets. Try those perennials or annuals which are not always too attractive in bush or plant but bear unforgettable blooms, like baby's breath, or the various everlasting flowers such as helichrysum, lunaria, and physalis (Chinese lantern), all of which can be dried for winter bouquets. The cutting garden is also an excellent spot to have reserve plants: those which can be lifted and transplanted to bare spots in your garden when more color is needed.

Annuals in round-form

African daisy	Marigold
Asters	Painted daisy
Bachelor's button	Pink
Calendula	Poppy
Calliopsis	Rudbeckia
Carnation	Scabiosa
Cosmos	Zinnia
Dahlia	

Annuals for height

Blue and red salvia	Heliotrope
Canterburhy bells	Larkspur
Cleome	Lupine
Columbine	Salpiglossis
Flowering tobacco	Snapdragon

Dainty-airy annuals

Baby's breath	Schizanthus
Forget-me-not	Statice
Love-in-mist	Tagetes

Container plants need more care

Colorful annuals growing in pots, tubs, boxes, hanging baskets, planters, and other containers will decorate and brighten the patio, terrace, or porch and add great warmth and cheer to the surroundings. Even in a backyard of concrete and gravel a sense of nature can be introduced and an outdoor living area developed.

Container-grown plants require more care than plants growing in the open ground. Their roots are confined to a smaller soil area from which they draw nutrients, and the soil will naturally dry out faster, so it is necessary to cultivate and water more frequently and regularly.

Because these plants are in containers, they are more conspicuous, they will need careful housekeeping. Faded flowers or discolored foliage must be removed daily and the plants must be kept at their best.

No patio is complete without the glamor of a few dramatic, colorful pot plants placed in strategic places for pictorial effects. The patio or terrace is an outdoor living room and should be made attractive and relaxing for family and friends. A fence on one side may give just the necessary privacy and also supply a background for vines and annuals.

Portable planters suit special occasions

The popular trend to more outdoor living has encouraged home owners to maintain mobile gardens, with annuals freely used to produce special effect for special occasions. Portable plant boxes and flower tubs can be equipped with casters to facilitate moving. You can also grow plenty of winter-blooming pansies to fill the tubs for winter, and plant some forget-me-nots and perennial Marguerites, which can be dug up in February and planted in the tubs to give loads of color from then until May or June, when the annuals go in.

Clay pots, wooden or concrete tubs, urns, and even old kettles and wine barrels, cut in half, are some of the many containers that can be used. They should be in scale with the surroundings and

115

large enough to put on a real show. Such containers will usually require larger and taller plants than the average sized window box.

Summer days can be a special joy on the patio, but even in the dreary days of winter a planter of bright blooming pansies can brighten the living room window. The summer patio planters bring color and fragrance. For the sunny spots, consider geraniums, lantana, marguerites, petunias, dusty miller, celosia, portulaca, salvia, and dwarf marigolds. For the shady areas, fuchsias, begonias, impatiens, coleus, caladium, and schizanthus.

Window boxes are also a tremendous asset, adding beauty and value to the home. A white house offers little difficulty in choosing a color scheme, but it can also act as a reflector, increasing the effects of both sun and shade. Yellow and orange marigolds with blue ageratum and lobelia against a white house with white sweet alyssum trailing over the edge of the box are effective as well as easy care. The combination of bright red Irene geraniums with blue trailing lobelia is another picture of beauty.

The containers, planters, or window boxes should be filled with a good soil mixture. My favorite mix is two parts soil mix and one part mushroom manure, both of which are readily available at the garden centers. For boxes or containers used the previous year, simply mix a healthy amount of mushroom manure into last year's soil mix. This will lighten the soil, giving it greater water retention and adding needed nutrients.

Don't forget, patio containers should be watered regularly. Do not allow them to dry. In hot summer weather, the containers may need a daily watering, preferably every morning. The containers, planters and baskets should also be fed regularly throughout the heavy blooming summer season. I use Hi-Sol and fish fertilizer alternatively every two weeks. I water the pots first, and, after the water has drained through, water once more with the liquid fertilizer.

Gentle planting pays off

I would rather put a 10-cent plant in a 25-cent hole, than a 25-cent plant in a 10-cent hole. Soil and soil preparation are important.

It isn't good enough to simply put the shovel through the surface and pop in a plant, hoping it will grow and bloom profusely.

Another common mistake is to assume that a heavy application of fertilizer will result in good soil.

In beds, borders, and planters, soil usually may be improved by working it and by adding fertilizer and peat moss, but, if the soil is very sandy or is filled with clay, or if the hardpan was surfaced when they dug your basement, you'll have to apply the elbow grease. I recommend that you apply a generous application of manure and mix it into the top 6 inches (15 centimeters) of soil. Lime shoud be added if your soil is too acid, and the usual rate of application is approximately 10 pounds (4.5 kg) per 500 square feet (50 square meters). A properly balanced fertilizer should also be added, such as Flower and Vegetable Food (4-10-10).

Compost, your own great soil bank

The gardener who alway has a rotted compost heap ready for use and another heap in the process of decomposition has created his own valuable soil bank. A compost bin or trench is made in a shady, inconspicuous spot in the garden. Throw in anything that will decay, and break the material down into humus; use grass clippings, weeds, healthy plant trash, and leaves. A 2- to 3-inch (5- to 7-centimeter) layer of soil is spread on each foot of waste or discarded vegetable matter, and a sprinkling of compost-maker or agricultrual lime is added to the top of each layer of soil. Slope the sides gently so that the heap is narrower at the top. Keep the heap moist to hasten decaying action. You may turn the heap in about 3 months, and in 6 to 9 months you'll have a heap of black valuable humus that will help grow anything.

Liming compost material makes fertile soil for next year's planting.

A compost box is easy to construct

Build yourself a compost box with no bottom; spread your lawn clippings and other organic wastes in the box. If a box is not used, then dig a shallow pit, 3 feet (90 centimeters) wide and of a convenient length. Keep the topsoil to one side—you'll need it later. Preferably the bottom 3 or 4 inches (7 or 10 centimeters)

COMPOST BOX CONSTRUCTION

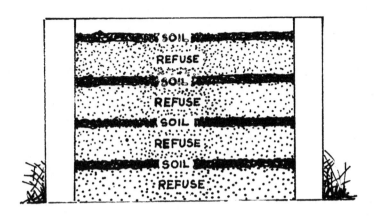

SOIL
REFUSE
SOIL
REFUSE
SOIL
REFUSE
SOIL
REFUSE

2 X 6 BOARDS

CONCRETE BRICKS

should be made up of coarse material, such as smashed cabbage stalks, because this will help to provide drainage. Spread a light dressing of white lime, sulphate of ammonia, or compost-maker over this, then add a 1-inch (2.5-centimeter) layer of soil. Build up the compost heap by repeating this procedure, but now make it with a 6-inch (15-centimeter) layer of waste; again repeat the lime, sulphate of ammonia, or compost-maker, but be sure the lime and sulphate of ammonia do not come in contact with each other. It is best to alternate the use of one or the other. If the heap becomes dry, water it. It takes about three months to make a fine batch of manure depending on the weather (it takes longer when the weather is cool.)

It is interesting to note that certain weeds are very beneficial to the compost heap. Stinging nettles speed the fermentation process, and not only do they contain a lot of beneficial iron, but they also have a certain carbon-nitrogen ratio. Dandelions absorb between 2 and 3 times as much iron from the soil as other weeds. Sheep sorrel take up phosphorus, buttercups accumulate potassium, horsetail contains plenty of cobalt, and thistles contain copper.

Do not let the weeds go to seed. Mow before seed develops and turn the remains into the compost.

Proper drainage is a must

Your planting areas must have adequate drainage. The roots of plants require air as well as moisture. Without it, they soon suffer and die, regardless of how rich the soil. That is why flower pots have drainage holes and why all tubs and window-boxes or planters must be provided with adequate drainage openings.

When choosing your garden plants, consider their light requirements. Some species thrive under average conditions, while other plants do well only in full sun, or, conversely, with considerable shade for protection. Don't grow your favorite plants where they are going to be unhappy.

120

A few favorites and where they belong

Portulaca gives a summer-long carpet of color under a blazing sun that would totally shrivel and scorch many other flowers.

Impatiens and coleus are gorgeously colored and offer a truly tropical showing in shaded locations, where most annuals would make only spindly growth with few blooms of inferior quality.

Care of annuals

Annuals are generally shallow-rooted and thus require regular watering. Water is best applied slowly over a sufficiently long period to penetrate to a depth of 6 inches (15 centimeters). Too many gardeners assume that, once planted, annuals can be left to their own resources. Compact, dwarf-growing plants take care of themselves very well; many others require pruning and training.

Pinching off the tips of young snapdragons and other tall growers just above a pair of upper leaves tends to produce bushy, self-supporting plants later on when they are loaded with blooms.

After a period of prolific bloom, the longer stems of most annuals, even the spreading types, may be cut back quite severely while removing faded blooms. This simply makes the bush flower all over again.

For hanging baskets in sun, try upright geranium, trailing geranium, nepeta, ice plant, gazania, and trailing lobelia, or a basket filled with cascading petunias.

For hanging baskets in shade, try fuchsias, begonias, impatiens, lobelia, and nepeta. The first three plants mentioned can be grown alone or each in combination with the last two.

For borders or edging, try ageratum, lobelia (rose, white, and blue), fibrous begonia (red, pink, and white), impatiens (red, pink, white or two-toned), salvia (red, white, or blue); and dwarf marigolds (all varieties). These will grow in full sun or partial shade.

Also good for borders in sunny spots are alyssum (white, pink and purple), ice plants (in all colors), verbena (all colors), petunia (double or single in all colors), phlox (mixed colors), and sweet william.

For cutting, try asters, carnations, celosia, cosmos, dahlia, stocks, snapdragons, or zinnias.

Vegetables for garden and patio

You don't need a large garden to produce a fine crop. Six hundred square feet (60 square meters) can produce enough to last a family of four all summer. In a condominium or appartment, which restricts you to a patio, you can effectively use pots, tubs, or planters. The planters, set in modular form, can make smart patterns. A 6-inch (15-centimeter) planter can be used for green onions, radishes, spinach, lettuce, parsley, chives, short rooted carrots, and all kinds of herbs. Planters can also be tiered.

In your pots and planters, use a rich soil mix. I prefer two parts black soil mixed with one part mushroom manure. The tubs will need to be kept fed throughout summer; use a liquid fish or Hi-Sol fertilizer about once every two weeks. Always keep plants well watered. If the vegetables dry out or begin to suffer for lack of food and stop growing, they may never come back.

The best vegetables to grow, whether in the garden or on the patio, are those eaten fresh. There's no point (if space is limited) in growing vegetables that require storing, as they can be purchased just as well in the store, but just after picking you can eat fresh radishes, lettuce, spinach, vine-ripened tomatoes, peas, and string beans, and corn so sweet it melts in your mouth.

All fruit producing vegetables like warm weather and plenty of sun. The leafy vegetables like it cool and enjoy shade.

Cool-weather plants must be planted in early spring so that they have as many cool days as possible, or in late summer for the same reason.

Perennial vegetables such as rhubarb, asparagus, and artichoke are cool-weather vegetables, and can also be grown as ornamentals.

Root crops prefer a loose soil, and all but potatoes return the greatest poundage per square foot.

Cole crops, or the cabbage family, including broccoli, Brussels sprouts, cauliflower, collards, kale, and kohlrabi are cool season growers and heavy feeders.

Try landscaping with vegetables

You can plant your pots, tubs, and planters with vegetables and still enjoy a lot of beauty and color.

Try scarlet runner beans against a stick frame in a large 24-inch (60-centimeter) pot. Grow clumps of beets and chard among flowers or straight in the pots. Rhubarb makes a very effective show, and you can even take the pot into the basement come winter and pick during the dreary late months of the year.

Flowering cabbage and kale make a tremendously colorful show in winter. Parsley and lettuce as greenery amongst colored marigolds are a super combination. Red cabbage in the planters or among the flowers gives a touch of something different.

The feathering foliage of asparagus at the back of a flowerbed or against the fence provides a look of tropical warmth. Try planting 12 kernels of sweet corn in a big tub placed on a sunny patio for a real tropical look.

Amazing asparagus

Asparagus is one of the most permanent and dependable of the home garden vegetables. Although the plants take 3 years to come into full production, they reward you for waiting by providing a seasonal crop for many years afterwards. Asparagus takes up a lot of space, but it does so in a stately manner; its tall, graceful growing habit makes it an ornamental beauty.

Asparagus is a perennial and cool season crop that produces from April to July, well ahead of other vegetables. It grows fence-high with many light branching stems; a long, narrow strip at the back of the property is worth planting with asparagus even if ordinary vegetable gardening is not your hobby.

You will find that it pays to buy crowns for planting, as growing from seed is a job for the experts.

Asparagus can be planted in spring or fall. It grows best in deep, loose, fertile soil prepared about 3 weeks before you plant the tips or crowns. You need roughly 200 square feet (20 square meters) for an asparagus bed containing two rows about 20 feet (6 meters) long set about 4 feet (1.2 meters) apart. This is large enough space to accommodate between 30 and 40 plants and is usually enough to supply a family of four, unless you really love it, as I do.

Dig trenches 8 inches (20 centimeters) wide, 20 feet (6 meters) long, and 6 to 8 inches (15 to 20 centimeters) deep. Work 4 inches (10 centimeters) of rotted manure into about 4 inches (10 centimeters) of the soil in the bottom of the trench. Set the asparagus crowns in the bottom of the trench so that the tops are between 6 and 8 inches (15 and 20 centimeters) below the top of the trench and the roots are spread out evenly. Space the crowns about 12 inches (30 centimeters) apart and cover with 2 inches (5 centimeters) of loose, pulverized soil. Water slowly and deeply.

As the young plants grow, fill in the trench little by little with loose soil, but don't cover the tips. By summer the trench will be completely filled.

A great taste treat—apple cabbage

In a 1980 article, I mentioned a great new find in the world of horticulture. Some say it's the greatest thing since sliced bread. The founders in Ipswich, England, Thompson and Morgan, Britain's formost seed company, were inundated with requests for this new vegetable development.

I'm told that never in the firm's entire 125-year history had any new seed caused greater interest the world over. Most major newspapers around the world carried stories lauding this new and great discovery.

It all started some 15 years ago when the seed company set out to develop a cross-breeding program that would make cabbage acceptable to the taste buds of youngsters, a cabbage that would taste simply great, cooked or raw.

The results of their research went beyond the greatest expectations of the developers: an easy-to-grow cabbage, which reaches the size of a basketball, matures early, keeps well, preserves tremendously, and, believe it or not, tastes like a Gravenstein apple when raw and has a deliciously different flavor when cooked.

Seed is now available at most garden centers and each package will produce 100 pounds (45 kilograms) or more of cabbage.

Consider nutrition when you choose vegetables

All gardeners know the obvious advantages of home grown produce.

Vegetables from the garden taste better and are fresher than the store bought variety. There's another benefit that should not be overlooked: you can grow crops in your garden that will never appear at your supermarket and will, at the same time, provide tremendous nutrition.

There are several ways to reap this high food value from your garden. They include choosing an especially nutritious variety, opting for a more nutritious alternative to the familiar vegetables, and eventually selecting for peak nutrition.

Beans   Green snap beans are about twice as high in Vitamin A content as are the yellow ones, although both are otherwise about equal in nutrients. Soybeans are a richer source of Vitamin A and are very high—10 per cent—in vegetable protein content. Soybeans are the most nutritious beans you can grow. If you're not too fond of soybeans, lima beans are a good second choice, being between green and yellow snap beans in Vitamin A, having about 7½ percent protein, and a good source of other nutrients.

Broccoli   Better than its cousin cauliflower in terms of some of the B vitamins and Vitamin C, broccoli contains about 40 times more Vitamin A. What is not generally recognized, though, is that broccoli leaves have several times as much Vitamin A by weight as do sprouts. Try cooking the tender young leaves of broccoli alone or with other cooking greens. Adding leafy stems and the apple-crisp core of the main stalk will provide more fiber as well. Old broccoli leaves are usually too tough to be cooking greens, but if you chop them and cook gently for about 15 minutes in a covered pan, the water will provide you with a good, nutritious soup stock.

Cabbage   Small heads of cabbage are often a more convenient size to deal with in the kitchen, and they have the nutritional advantage of containing more Vitamin C. Close spacing of your plants in the garden will produce smaller heads. Good small cabbage varieties include early Jersey wakefield, Jersey queen, and the midget dwarf morden. Another point to consider when choosing cabbage is the color; the deeper the green, the greater the nutritional value.

Carrots   These vegetables are a super source of Vitamin A, and there are two easy ways to increase that value. Harvest your carrots late, and plant the danvers and imperator varieties. Danvers is best, and it triples its Vitamin A content to 38,000 international units in $3\frac{1}{2}$ ounces (99 grams) when allowed to grow a few weeks beyond its normal 75 days maturity time.

Dandelion   The leaves are good food, and people who hate dandelions in their lawns should consider cultivating a taste for them. The leaves are one of the best sources of Vitamin A in existence. They are too bitter for some tastes when eaten raw but become milder when cooked, either alone or with some other greens such as chard. The real dandelion fancier may want to grow his own rather than relying on the lawn, and seed of a thick kind are available. Like curled endive, a dandelion's heart can be blanched by gathering the leaves together and tying; however, this removes some of the vitamins along with some of the bitterness. You should have no trouble growing dandelions; they do well in our area.

Lettuce   The leafy or butter-type lettuce contains the most vitamins. They are also some of the best eating. The butterhead lettuce is far more nutritional than the iceberg vareity. The darker green the lettuce, the higher it is in nutrition and vitamin content.

Melons   Cantaloupes, honeydews, and watermelons are more than just a delicious treat; they're good for you. Honeydews are by far the most nutritious, with an especially high level of Vitamin A and more Vitamin C than tomatoes. Watermelons have a good deal of Vitamin A. Cantaloupes, with their deep orange flesh, hold the highest amount of Vitamin A.

Peas   A surprisingly good source of vegetable protein, over 5 percent, peas are also high in vitamin content. This applies to the standard green peas. Edible podded-peas, also called sugar peas, sugar crisp, or snow peas, are superior in most nutrients to green snap beans.

Potatoes   They're not only delicious when eaten soon after digging them, but their Vitamin C level is then at its peak—about equal to that of green peas.

Sweet corn   This vegetable is a good source of vegetable protein and of the important B vitamins thiamine, riboflavin, and niacin.

Sweet peppers   They're good for you, both cooked or raw, and can be eaten at any stage of growth. For the greatest food value, let some peppers ripen on the plant until they turn a striking red color.

Tomatoes   They're good sources of Vitamin A and C, no matter what variety you grow.

Turnips   The root part is fairly nutritious, but turnip greens (leaves) are outstanding. They are 3 times as high in Vitamin C and about 10 times as high in Vitamin A as soybeans. They are also the vegetable source of Vitamin B12. Wash turnip greens briefly and cook them quickly in a covered pan. The moisture

127

from the rinsing will supply all the water needed. This goes for other leafy greens too.

Finally, a word about Vitamin C (ascorbic acid). It is soluble in water and thus more fleeting than other nutrients. Therefore don't soak fresh vegetables when washing them, and, if you're not planning to use them at once, store them in the fridge. This will also help retain other nutrients.

Incidentally, if hay fever bothers you, Vitamin C can be helpful.

Lots of sun, fertile soil, plenty of water, and the help of bees produce big zucchini.

On tomatoes and cucumbers, the salad elites

Everyone with a little space to spare and the itch to grow something loves to grow a vegetable that springs to life quickly and produces in great quantity.

Most backyard gardeners will try their luck with cucumbers and tomatoes this year and will probably be fairly successful, yet there is some very basic know-hows that every gardener should learn in the growing of these two vegetables.

Growing cucumbers

If you are starting your plants from seed, soak the seeds overnight. Start them indoors in small pots with starter mix soil or sow directly outside when night temperatures are sufficiently warm for quick germination. You can also purchase plants already started, and just a few will provide adequate produce for the average household. Whatever you do, be sure to plant in pockets about 12 inches (30 centimeters) square, filled with a mixture of compost or mushroom manure and soil. Plant about 18 inches (45 centimeters) apart, and be sure to sprinkle a little slug bait around your plants, or you could lose your efforts overnight.

When sowing directly outdoors, put three seeds 1 inch (2.5 centimeters) deep and a few inches (8 to 10 centimeters) apart in manure and soil. Plant about 18 inches (45 centimeters) apart, and be sure to sprinkle a little slug bait around your plants, or you could lose your efforts overnight.

When sowing directly outdoors, put three seeds 1 inch (2.5 centimeters) deep and a few inches (8 to 10 centimeters) apart in the center of each pocket, and, after good germination, thin out the weakest, leaving the strongest plants to mature. It takes about 9 days for germination, and from sowing to picking normally requires three months. You can safely expect about 2 dozen good-sized cucumbers per plant. You'll need a sunny spot and a well-drained soil rich in humus.

With cucumbers, pinch out the growing tips when the plants have developed 6 to 7 leaves. Lateral shoots will then develop,

One of my favorite varieties of tomato is Balls Extra Early.

Plenty of sun, water, and feed produce a bumper crop of tomatoes.

and these can be left on the ground or trained up netting. Any lateral shoot not bearing fruit should be pinched out at the seventh leaf.

Keep the soil moist. Water around the plants, not over them, but spray lightly in dry weather. Once the fruit starts to swell, protect it from contact with the soil with a piece of wood. When fruit develops, start feeding with a liquid fertilizer.

Never remove the male flowers; fertilization is essential.

Don't try to grow record-breaking fruits. They should be cut before they reach maximum size for best flavor and to encourage new fruit to set.

The most popular varieties are Chicago pickling, straight eight, or long green.

Keep plenty of slug bait around your cucumbers, and watch for mice. Lots of sunshine and plenty of ventilation will help prevent fungus, but a good fungicide may be required several times during the growing season.

Growing tomatoes

Almost everyone loves home-grown tomatoes. Choose a warm spot in front of a south-facing wall, if you can. Generously work compost or mushroom manure into the soil and sprinkle in some tomato food at the time of planting. You can also grow tomatoes in pots. The patio tomato and Tiny Tim cherry tomato are particularly popular for this. The pot should be 9 to 12 inches (22 to 30 centimeters) deep, filled with a good soil-manure mix; tomatoes in pots will require more regular watering and feeding.

You may wish to raise your own seedlings, but the majority of gardeners find they have more success by purchasing young plants. When planting young seedlings, plant somewhat deeper than they were planted in their original containers at the time of purchase. My favorite trick is to plant on an angle, burying half the plant so that it may root all along the stem, giving it real growing power. This normally requires removal of all but the top leaves; don't worry about the angle when planted, the plant will

131

CONTAINER TOMATOES

TIE LOOSLY TO
STAKE FOR
SUPPORT

soon straighten up and result in an upright, sturdy plant.

If you are growing the bush varieties, you will not need to concern yourself with staking. However, most gardeners select the regular varieties, and you should loosely tie the stem to a cane or stick. Make the ties at 12-inch (30-centimeter) intervals as the plant grows.

Side shoots will appear where the leaf stalks join the stem. Cut or pinch them out when they are about 1 inch (2.5 centimeters) long. Yellowing leaves below a ripening truss should also be removed, but never overdo the defoliating.

When small tomatoes appear on the fourth truss, remove the tip at two leaves above this truss.

Aim to keep the soil moist; alternating dryness with flooding will lead to blossom rot and drop, as well as fruit split. Feed regularly with tomato food. Spray occasionally, and sprinkle with tomato and potato dust to prevent insects and disease.

Pick the fruit when ripe and fully colored, except when frost threatens, at which time any remaining fruit should be gathered and ripened on the window sill. When picking the fruit, snap the stalk off the stem so that the calyx remains on the tomato.

With tomatoes, let me stress again, watch for slugs, cutworm, or woodlice. Apply tomato and potato dust from shortly after planting until almost picking time.

A common problem, blossom drop, is generally due to lack of pollination. A blossom set will help, but so will simply tapping the plants to distribute the pollen. Regular watering and spraying the flowers in the morning also prevents blossom drop.

Dandelions for breakfast

Scientists and those seeking to make a fast buck in new products have long been looking to find a substitute for expensive coffees.

I've discovered a recipe worth trying. It's made from *Taraxacum officinale*, better know as the dandelion. There's plenty of it about and no matter how long and hard we harvest, there will always be more.

The dandelion is a relative of chicory (succory), the coffee weed. Collect the roots, and don't worry about having other plants for next year, since a small root particle left in the soil produces a whole new plant. Clean the dandelion roots and dry roast them in the oven at 200°F (92°C) for up to 4 hours, until they snap crisply and are dark brown inside. Grind them to a powder in a blender or coffee mill and store this powder in a jar. For 8 cups, put a half cup of the powder plus a pinch of salt in a percolator basket and brew as you would coffee. Since it's a potent drink, you may want to add cream and sugar.

Q: Last year my roses produced only small leaves, pale green and with little red spots. Why?
A: Your roses lack nitrogen. Apply a compound fertilizer this year.

Q: How long should a hydrangea bloom in the house?
A: It should flower for not less than 3 weeks. Keep it away from a hot, sunny window or heaters, and water each day.

Q: Will a pot hydrangea bloom again?
A: Yes. Cut back a bit after bloom is finished and keep well watered until May. In May, plant pot and all or bigger pots outside in a sunny spot. Feed and water to encourage new growth. Bring indoors before a hard frost and induce a rest period by coolness and very little water. Start up again in January. Give full light but little water at first. Temperature should never be above 15°C (60°F).

Q: Can my hydrangea be planted in the garden permanently after it has finished blooming in the house?
A: Yes. After blooming, cut back the stems about half the length, remove plant from pot, and plant in the garden where it will have plenty of room. It will grow into a big, sturdy plant. Water well.

Given a choice, I would prefer to buy a regular outdoor variety, however.

Q: **What elements make the hydrangea blue?**
A: Acidity of soil causes blue flowers, but some varieties come blue more readily than others. Repeated watering with alum solution or magnesium sulfate (1 level teaspoon to 1 gallon or 4 liters of water) will produce bluer blooms.

Q: **Last year I purchased some roses that were supposed to be very fragrant but I was disappointed in a number of these. Can you tell me why the lack of fragrance?**
A: Some roses have more fragrance than others, but none will be as fragrant in cold or wet weather, as in warm.

Q: **Some of my roses have seven leaves; are they wild?**
A: Some plants naturally produce leaves having seven leaflets; therefore, it is sometimes assumed that any branch having seven instead of five is wild and should be cut back. The rule is, any branch or root that starts out from below the bud union or graft is a "sucker" and these should be removed.

Q: **My rose blooms are sometimes a better color than others and vary somewhat from those my cousin has. Why?**
A: Off-color blooming is a temporary condition and can be caused by many things. New plants are more apt to be affected. Usually the true color doesn't come forth till the second year. Weather may affect the color, and blooms produced in spring will vary from the blooms produced in fall.

Q: **I spend hours picking the curly leaves off my peach trees. What causes them to curl?**
A: Your task is next to impossible. There is no cure—only prevention. Peach leaf curl is a fungus that develops over winter, with the spores developing through the winter rains. If you could plant your peach tree out of the rain—under cover—you would have no curl and no sun either, so the best way to prevent curl is

through a spray application of copper spray or lime sulphur and dormant oil during winter. But for now, after picking off all those curly leaves, spray with benomyl and fish fertilizer.

Q: My rhododendron has mottled leaves and looks rusty. The leaves seem to curl downwards. What can I do to improve the looks?

A: Mottled foliage and a rusty brown below would indicate possible infestation of rhododendron bug—shiny brown insects with lacy wings. The curling downward of leaves is further indication of bug infestation. Spray with Malathion—2 tablespoons (40 ml) per gallon (4 liters) of water and add 2 tablespoons (40 ml) of fish fertilizer as a sticker.

Q: A number of our coniferous trees have a snow or cotton like stuff on them and our Japanese cherry tree has leaves with brown spots and holes in the leaves. What can we do?

A: Well, in May that certainly isn't snow on those coniferous trees—those "tufts" of white wool, usually on the underside of the trees are caused by woolley aphids. Spray with Malathion and fish fertilizer as I prescribed above for rhododendron bugs. Repeat in 3 weeks. For your Japanese maple, it's probably infected with shothole disease. Spray with Benomyl fungicide and apply a generous feeding of tree food fertilizer—only weak trees are attacked.

Q: I want a tall, fast-growing hedge for a place really wet most of the time. What should I choose?

A: Try hemlock—it should do well.

Q: Some funny little scaly things seem to be taking over my filbert bush. Is this harmful and what should I do to remove them?

A: Those strange little scalelike creatures are called oyster scale. Because they multiply so quickly and suck all the life-giving juices from your trees, you should act quickly. Spray with 2 tablepsoons of Orthene, Lagon, Latox, or Cygon mixed in 1 gallon (4 liters) of water and, to make the spray stick, add 2 tablespoons (40 ml) of fish fertilizer. Read the label of whatever spray you obtain.

June

When nature's tap keeps running

Rain, rain, and more rain! Vegetable gardens and flower beds suffer with the long stretches of rain and cool nights we often experience during June in the northwest, especially in the coastal areas.

Sooner or later, the sun will appear and stay on duty most of the summer, and our plants will take off like a house afire. There is nothing like a moist, fertile soil, the right season, and good warm sunshine to make up for lost time. Just watch those poor peas and beans, which have been crying out for a little heat, push ahead.

June is what I call watchdog month. Gardeners have to keep after insects and pests, nurture young plants, and look after the shrubs which have completed their blooms.

Stop those slugs

During June's backward days, begonias will show little progress, but after a few warm days you won't recognize them. Until they take off, keep the weeds out and don't allow those pesky slugs (which appear in battalions, it seems) to devour your young seedlings. Our little plants make luscious and quick eating for a slug's evening meal. I always use slug bait around the starting plants, and, when it's cooler and wetter than usual, I double the dosage. After all the hard work of preparing the soil, digging, and planting, I'm not about to start all over again for lack of a little slug bait.

What to do about unwanted mushrooms

If you've noticed a dandy crop of mushrooms popping up across your lawn, and they're not the edible kind, there are two forms of attack. If the problem is great, it may be necessary to get out the fungicide or apply a high magnesium fertilizer. But if you have a small problem, just knock the tops off the toadstools before they spread their spores. Rake the area with a steel rake to take out some of the thatch, which is the medium on which they thrive. Then punch some holes in the infested area to allow for better drainage. This also allows air to get into the surrounding ground.

Look after your prize rhododendrons

Every northwest garden should have at least one rhododendron. It's one of our most beautiful flowering shrubs, and it's little wonder that Washington State adopted it as the official state flower.

Now's the time for some care to ensure next year's success. Carefully remove the old blooms with your thumb and forefinger. Care must be taken not to remove the leaf buds that sit at the base of the old blooms unless, of course, you wish to stop or slow the overall growth of the rhododendron. In this case, removing new leaf buds is the way to shape the shrub or slow growth.

Moles, grubs, and other crawly things

I once had a little mole friend that became a real pest; he was determined to dig along my front walkway, leaving a trail of unsightly earth mounds all over the front part of my lawn.

Moles are nearly blind but they have a supersensitive sense of hearing. You can control them by creating a noise that is offensive. To do this, bury old wine bottles in the mole runs with the necks sticking out at angles. This is not merely an old wives' tale. It works! The wind passing over the open bottles sends noise through the runs and the moles leave the area.

Sometimes, however, a more effective remedy is needed. The moles are there in the first place because they are after grubs in your soil. When I set out to catch the little night raider, I discovered a fair number of leatherjacket grubs. These grubs eat the young grass roots, the moles eat the grubs, but unfortunately do not move quickly enough to keep up with the spread of the leatherjacket population.

To get rid of the grubs and deny the mole his feast, use Diazinon at the rate of 2 tablespoons (40 ml) per gallon (4 litres) of water, applied by a watering can at the rate of 1 gallon (4 liters) every 200 square feet (20 square meters).

Many people are troubled with cutworms, slugs, and grubs that destroy young pepper and tomato plants. I always suggest sprinkling Diazinon granules around the plants to ward off the little marauders until the plants are strong enough to withstand the attacks.

Fuchsias are vigorous, consistent bloomers

Growing fuchsias is a relatively new hobby. Back in the '20s the only fuchsias were a shrubby lot of unexciting varieties of small red and purple flowers. In the '30s new hybrids were brought over from England. Soon, various California breeders began cross-pollinating the best existing varieties. Before long breathtaking colors and startling forms began to appear. The rebirth of the lowly fuchsia had taken place.

The new fuchsias aren't merely improvements over old-timers; they represent distinct advances in color, habit, and all-round performance. All of the new ones are vigorous and consistent bloomers through summer and fall. Today's fuchsias come in a wide range of scarlets, lovely pinks, soft salmons and oranges, striking bicolors, and pure white.

The versatile fuchsias can be used in scores of ways: as potted plants, standards, hanging baskets, and a variety of trained arrangements such as climbing.

Most fuchsias require partial shade, although some will do reasonably well in the sun. The north or east side of a building or wall is fine. A spot under high-branched trees whose canopy of foliage provides protection against the hot afternoon sun is ideal.

It's easy to root fuchsia cuttings. Make a clean cut above the leaf union.

Practically all fuchsias like cool, summer weather. That's the main reason for their success in our area. Regular (daily, in warm weather) overhead waterings not only help growth but repel invasions of white flies, aphids, and red spider.

Fuchsias can be put out anytime after about the middle of April, but even in June and July they can be started in baskets and planters, and will grow quickly.

Fuchsias succeed in almost any reasonably good garden soil. A rich, fibrous mixture consisting of two parts garden loam, one part peat moss and one part mushroom manure is ideal. Such a mixture is porous and drains rapidly. At this time, it may be well to mulch with a 2 inch thich (5 centimeters) layer of mushroom manure around the base of the plant. This keeps the roots cool, the moisture in, the weeds down, and feeds at the same time.

Fuchsias love water. Give them plenty during the hotter weather. The combination of proper soil and frequent watering and a good feeding schedule makes them bloom. As mentioned earlier, fuchsias don't mind water on the leaves, even at night. They actually love it.

Since the flowers are borne on the current season's growth, do all you can to feed and force out new branches. My wife Lillian and I have a favorite feeding recipe. Never feed a dry plant. We water a few hours or even half-a-day before feeding. We feed once every two or three weeks in June, July, August, and September and cut back all feeding after that.

Our feeding mix is two tablespoons (40 ml) of liquid fish fertilizer and one level teaspoon (20 ml) of Hi-Sol (20-20-20) to one gallon (4 liters) of water. We use tepid water or mix up a batch and let it stand, then stir and use when required. Last year the fuchsias bloomed until the end of November.

Fortunately, fuchsias are relatively free from the usual list of pests and diseases. Yet aphids, mealybugs, and white flies do attack the plants occasionally, but, with good feeding and watering, I have gone a whole summer and fall without any spraying at all. When I do spray, I use insecticidal soap, malathion, pyrethrin or rotenone. Some fuchsia lovers spray every two weeks with insecticidal soap, taking care to spray the underside of the leaves also. They use an easy trigger sprayer and thus prevent any bugs from taking hold.

If you want to take some cuttings of your own, use softwood cuttings from green, soft, leafy branches. They should be about 3 inches (8 centimeters) long. Select wood from the most actively growing, leafiest branches. Cut with a sharp knife through the soft, green immature stems.

Good practices will prolong color display in your garden

The usual life pattern of an annual is to grow, flower, set seed, and die—all in one season. They are free bloomers, but there is a point in their life cycle when tissues begin to harden, growth stops, and seed development begins.

Hot weather often hardens the tissues prematurely. This is why annuals in our coastal region bloom longer than in the hotter interior areas. Tissues also harden if the supply of nutrients gives out before the plant is mature. Lack of water and damage to the plant by disease or garden pests are further contributing factors.

Anything you, the gardener, can do to prevent annuals from completing the cycle of producing seeds will prolong their bloom. Even after natural hardening has started, you can still encourage more flowers to develop by removing faded blooms. This prevents the development of seeds. To forestall premature hardening of the tissues and prolong the blooming season of annuals, consider this advice.

Select annuals suited to your climate. Nasturtiums, for example, grow very well in cool climates, as do marigolds, while zinnias and petunias do better where the weather is warmer.

Feed annuals almost as soon as they are in the ground. Regular once-a-month feeding is not too often. Water deeply and repeat whenever the top 1 or 2 inches (2.5 to 5 centimeters) of soil dries out. No need to worry when there's been plenty of rain, but once the showers end, check your annuals often.

Rotovate, using a rake or pronghoe between plants, being careful not to disturb the roots. The loosened soil acts like a mulch, keeping down the weeds and keeping in the moisture.

Control pests and diseases. Sweet peas will bloom 4 to 6 weeks longer if not allowed to mildew. The same applies to our popular calendulas and zinnias.

Keep faded blooms picked off. Make this a regular chore, daily if possible. Annuals that produce heavy masses of flowers early in the season will wear themselves out and die back unless all seed pods are removed before they mature. This can become quite a task with flowers such as poppies, which develop seeds rapidly, but I never touch my fibrous begonias and they carry on blooming like crazy. They are my favorite bedding plant.

The amount of fertilizer used should be determined by the soil, its previous treatment, and the requirements of the top. The idea with annuals is to keep them growing fast. The all-purpose Feed-All 6-8-6 fertilizer with iron is one that can be used very successfully, and an application of fish fertilizer is also very effective. A good program is to feed about once a month and alternate 6-8-6 with liquid fish fertilizer.

Always work or rake the fertilizer into the soil, and then add water to dissolve it. Fertilizer must be soluble in water to be available to the plants. In general, use 2 to 3 pounds (1 to 1.5 kilograms) of fertilizer for every 100 square feet (10 square meters), one-third at the time of planting, one-third when first growth starts, and one-third just as the plants begin to bloom. Never over-use fertilizer, as this can do much harm. Follow the instructions on the bag.

I prefer to apply the fertilizer by hand. Apply along the sides of the rows, being careful to keep the fertilizer off the foliage. I sprinkle overhead after the feeding to wash off any that may have fallen on the leaves.

Light sprinklings do more harm than good. Deep watering encourages deep roots. When the plants are in full bloom, ground watering is preferred over sprinkling, but, again, my fibrous begonias don't seem to mind either way. Early morning watering is usually the best for all gardens.

Preventive steps will help stop pests

Annuals are comparatively free from attacks by garden pests, since their short life tends to discourage a build-up in insect population.

Two factors that will encourage trouble should be noted. Annuals grown with other plants already infested will soon become infested. A single variety grown in large numbers in the same spot year after year may also run the risk of trouble.

FERTILIZER APPLICATION

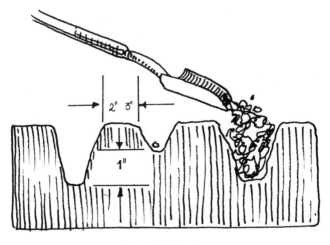

IN ROWS BESIDE SOWN ROWS

HOE DIRECTLY INTO SOIL

You can avoid this problem by taking the following preventive steps.

Healthy plants build up a resistance to attack. Weak plants are susceptible.

Maintain good housekeeping and clean, sanitary practices. Keep down the weeds, remove yellowed leaves or stems, and destroy by burning any diseased or infested parts.

Rotate susceptible plants with non-susceptible ones.

Provide well-prepared soil and adequate drainage.

Maintain a good, well-balanced, and nutritional soil.

Allow for plenty of light and air among the foliage.

Keep soil rich between plants by a light rotating or a mulch, such as "garden mix" or steer manure.

Spray or dust as necessary to prevent the spread of disease or insects to other plants.

When using any insecticide or fungicide, be sure to read the label before applying to plants, and use no more than necessary.

Slug baits should be put out early. If you do not like the conventional slugbaits, use a liquid spray. This is especially good if there are small pets around.

All dusts and sprays are poisonous to a certain degree. Beware of the dangers that lie in careless handling of these compounds.

To best combat a particular insect or disease, one must be able to at least partially recognize the culprit. You should know what you are attempting to cure before you decide on the medicine. Here is a partial list of the most common garden problems and the products most often recommended for combat.

Aphids   These plant lice live on plants and suck the plant's juices, causing curled and distorted leaves. Aphids are one of the main carriers of virus diseases, so get rid of them. Use an insecticide such as Malathion, Rotenone, or Pyrethrin. These recommended insecticides should not be purchased in large quantities and stored over from year to year, as they will lose their strength.

Beetles   Brown or black Asiatic and Japanese beetles, and thin, long, blister beetles damage certain plants such as asters, calendula, cosmos, and dahlias by eating the foliage. They often feed at night. Use sevin dust for best control of these pests.

Cutworms   These insects chew off the plant near the surface of the ground. Dust the soil with diazinon dust or sprinkle with diazinon granules.

Leafhoppers   These winged, leaping insects suck the juice of plants. They love to attack the underside leaves of dahlias, and they carry viruses. Spray with Malathion.

Leaf miners   These are chewing insects that make tunnels in the leaves. Again, use Malathion.

Mealybugs   These sucking insects are covered with a white, woolly protective substance, and are found at the joints and underside of leaves. They suck the juices from the stems and leaves, stunting growth and killing the plants. If only a few mealybugs are present, pick them off with a toothpick or kill them with a swab of cotton or a matchstick dipped in rubbing alcohol. Spray with Malathion.

Stalk borers   These 1-inch-long (2.5 centimeters) striped grey caterpillars tunnel or burrow into the stems of flower stalks. Spray with Malathion.

Thrips   These are minute insects which cause flowers to be malformed and blotched with brown or white. Spray with Malathion.

Whitefly   This is a small, white, winged, sucking insect that attacks the underside of leaves and lays eggs there. Leaves of infested plants become pale, mottled, or stippled; the plants lack vigor, turn yellow, and die. Leaves become sticky with honeydew and often are coated with black sooty mold. Spray with insecticide soap or Malathion.

Mites   Red spider mite is the most common and destructive. Red spider mites are minute but can often be seen with the naked eye when they move. They thrive in hot, dry weather and multiply rapidly in favorable conditions. They usually live on the underside of leaves and buds in a flimsy web. Infested leaves develop a mottled yellow appearance with stunted growth. Frequent applications of insecticidal soap or Malathion will keep them in check.

Nematodes   These tiny eelworms tunnel through the feeding roots, causing irregular swellings or nodules. Infested plants are stunted, weak in growth, and pale green. If infested, discard the whole plant.

Botrytis   This grey mold forms on the infected plants. Cut away infected parts and burn, and reduce watering. Use a copper spray.

Mildew   This thin, dirty-white mass of growth forms on the leaves, stems, and buds. Use Benomyl or Funginex.

Mosaic disease   This is a virus disease characterized by mottling of the foliage. Use Benomyl.

Nature needs a helping hand with city lawns

The most important ingredient for proper growth of any plant is water. We all know that, without it, plants dry up. Too much water, on the other hand, tends to make them bloated. Water will do the same for your grass, making it fat, weak, soft, and susceptible to disease and damage. The secret is to water properly.

There's no doubt that you can't beat rain water. Even my slightly polluted waterhole can't produce the healthy growth that one can expect from a good rain shower. During an electrical storm, the rain particles are charged with as much as 75 percent nitrogen, which accounts for the fresh, green look of a lawn after a thunder storm.

Next to rain water, directly from the sky, I prefer to treat my lawn with water from my waterhole. The water comes from surface run-off, especially good after a downpour. It is fed by normal drainage, but its reliability as a continuing water source stems from underground springs. This is not unlike my well water, except that it probably has more nitrogen and less iron.

Lawn watering tips

The least desirable choice is what most people have to contend with: city tap water. Our city tap water lacks the nitrogen and many other natural elements, but does contain some added chemicals, particularly chlorine and salt. I'm not convinced that chlorine in such small quantities is in any way bad for your plants or lawn, but the salts are definitely not helpful. Who would ever water with salt? Yet we do, and right from the tap. Fortunately, the northwest's public water supply is probably the best on the continent.

The best time to water is just after sunrise. While the dew is still on the lawn, turn on your sprinkler and water. Allow your hose to run so that you'll get deep penetration. Deep water penetration means deep roots and deep roots mean strength. Shallow watering encourages shallow rooting. The roots will stay closer to the surface of the soil and, therefore, be much more prone to drying out, should you miss watering. When the shallow roots dry up, the rhizome is injured, the top of the plant dies, and soon you have a brown lawn.

The reason for early watering is to permit the lawn to dry out slowly by the time evening comes. If the lawn goes to bed wet, there's a great probability that fungi or other lawn diseases may set in. The top of the grass is cool, and the earth down inside stays warm. The fertilizer, which has nitrogen in it, makes the soil warm. So, if you add the water in the late afternoon, you create ideal incubating conditions for lawn diseases. It sure helps in growing a mushroom crop as well.

My friend might argue this because the golf course where he works always waters during the night hours; but he forgets that we at home don't collect green fees and we don't have to consider early morning golfers when we turn on our sprinklers. Besides that, the golf course spends a great deal of money spraying with fungicides, probably once every week.

Lawn feeding a must

People often ask what I feed my lawn to keep it green and healthy. Nature provides a lot of nutrients from the soil and air, but nature didn't intend that plants grow as close and be as productive as we demand. So we must give our plants extra food. In summer I use a 13-5-7 or 10-6-4 at the rate of about 50 pounds (23 kilograms) to every 3000 to 4000 square feet (270 to 360 square meters). I apply it in June and again in early August. Lawn Treat, which has an analysis of 13-5-7, has four sources of nitrogen, and thus is a slow-release and long-lasting fertilizer. I do not use Weed-and-Feed, as that's a little like a Corn Flakes diet: it helps for a little while, but you're hungry again shortly after.

If I find I have a crop of weeds, I use liquid Weed-All weed-killer at the rate of 2 tablespoons (40 ml) per gallon (4 liters) of water, and I apply it only where I have weeds, with a watering can on a warm day. This way, I don't have to worry about burning my lawn or putting a lot of chemicals where they aren't needed.

Some tips on mowing

You can't mow wet grass. Grass with water on it will mash under the mower wheels, stick to the blades, and slither away from the cutting machine. Best to wait until the lawn dries, unless you can knock the water off the blades with a sweeper, brooms, or piece of burlap. This would be a little difficult in the glorious northwest during some of the prolonged rainy spells, but it's a task that may be necessary if you are trying to impress your visiting cousins from Vegreville, Alberta or Tucson, Arizona.

Stop! Don't pile those clippings

Never simply put grass clippings on a pile. A pile of grass clippings may appear to be harmless, but it isn't. It breeds flies. As many as 3000 housefly larvae (maggots) have been found in a single small pile of decomposing grass. The two most common pests to breed are the regular housefly and the lesser housefly. The regular housefly is the one that flies a little and then lands on a table to rest and fly again. The lesser housefly is the little one that flies around and around the living room and seldom lands.

It doesn't take long for flies to develop in piled grass. Adult flies can emerge from a breeding place in as little as 7 days after the eggs are laid, and this can all occur in grass clippings piled only 3 inches (7½ centimeters) deep.

Scatter clippings over your compost pile. If you don't have a compost area, now is a good time to start, although the best time is in early spring when you can start the process of rotting all those weeds you pulled.

Q: **My strawberries taste flat, though they used to be tasty. Why?**
A: Chances are the soil is too sweet. Add peat moss and manure to increase acidity.

Q: **The edges of my sycamore tree and lilac bush leaves have turned brown and are now beginning to fall off. Can you give me a reason for this?**
A: Anthracnose is the cause of your trouble. It's a fungus disease brought on by lots of rain. Spray in winter, during dormant season, with copper spray and repeat the operation after new leaves appear in spring, using Funginex or Benomyl the second spraying time.

Q: **We've just moved into a new house and the big fir tree left in the front yard appears to be dying. Why?**
A: Probably dirt has been bulldozed against the trunk of the tree

and now the tree can't breathe properly. Dig away the dirt to where it used to be or else dig a well about three feet in diameter around the tree.

Q: Why did my father in the Kootenays paint the trunks of fruit trees white and what did he use?
A: He used white hydrated lime, made it into a soup, and painted it on with a brush. It keeps ants and insects from climbing up and boring through the bark.

Q: I've got spit on my rosebushes—how come?
A: Well, it's not spit as such, so don't blame the neighbor's kids. Inside the spit (remove some with your thumb and forefinger) you'll find some fat little green bugs. These are spittle bugs, so your term wasn't far off. They may not be as damaging as some other rose insects, but they're a nuisance and look bad. Spray with Orthene or Latox.

Q: When should I cut down a yucca candle?
A: As soon as it's done blooming. The yucca (or Lord's candle) is a lovely and versatile evergreen that does well in the northwest.

Q: How do I dry bittersweet?
A: Hang it upside down in the sun.

Q: What can I do about the neighbor's dog ruining my lawn?
A: I know what you would like to do, but being a dog and cat lover I can't recommend it. Dog damage or urine burn can be repaired by applying a handful of white agricultural lime to the affected area after scratching up the soil, and then reseeding. To prevent this damage, you can apply white lime to the entire lawn in spring and fall, thus discouraging repeated visits by the neighbor's dog. There are also dog and cat repellent pellets available that can be sprinkled on the trouble spots in summer.

July

A warning about sudden heat

At the risk of disturbing those in the tourist bureaus, we in the northwest must admit we sometimes have rather wet springs extending into early summer. Often, it seems the rain just won't quit, especially when we've had a warm, promising early spring.

In July, the sun and heat will cause the plants to grow quickly; they try to make up for lost time and effort.

There is some danger with plants that have grown too lanky or spindly and are loaded with water. The sudden turn to heat and sun could cause many of your favorites to wither and die. I would recommend that you shade any of the less hardy plants for just a couple of days to make the transition a little more gradual.

A walk through my garden

I'm going to wander through the garden with you in order to provide a few tips that are timely for summer and, at the same time, urge you to read the question and answer section at the end of the chapter.

As I walk out the front door, I see a lovely display of fuchsia baskets down my walkway. They've experienced a lot more flower drop than normal. This is due to the wet, dark weather. The fuchsias, though lovers of partial shade, do not like the continual cold, constant moisture, and they need sunlight at least part of the time.

My swingtime fuchsia, which is a favorite double red and white, has flowers which are not as bright as those of previous years, due to the cool, damp summer days and nights. If we experience a slow-starting summer, during the first week of July I give the baskets a feeding of Hi-Sol, which is a pink powder 20-20-20 formulation that dissolves in liquid. Always, the thing to remember with your hanging baskets is that despite the continued rain, there isn't enough water getting into those baskets. You still need to get out there with the watering can every 3 or 4 days, depending on the number of plants in the baskets and the size of the basket, and give them a thorough soaking.

Remember also that you must not feed a dry basket. Give your container a good watering and then an hour or two later, water with the fertilizer mixture.

If you feed a dry basket, you'll burn the roots. The leaves quickly show signs of scorching. I turn my baskets once a week to give all sides a better chance at the light.

Out on the lawn, there has appeared a crop of mushrooms. They certainly don't look very attractive stretched in patches of white across an otherwise lush green carpet. A toadstool or mushroom is the fruiting body of a type of fungus. The actual vegetative portion of the mushroom is mycelium, a filament of underground growth. The mycelium grows on organic matter such as rotten wood in the lawn, or more likely, on old grass clippings.

Mushrooms sometimes grow in an expanded circle called fairy ring. Sometimes in the ring the mycelium or underground mushroom growth is so thick that water and air cannot get through to the grass roots, and the grass either suffers temporarily or dies completely. The mycelium inside the circle deteriorates as the circle expands, and this deterioration can supply nutrients to the grass, thus making the inside of the circle a brighter green.

Another problem which exists sometimes on my lawn is isolated colonies of mushrooms. This occurs when we have a cool season. The mushrooms in my lawn look unsightly and are poisonous so I want to get rid of them. The most popular remedies are to spray the area with mushroom killer or to poke holes in the ground where the mushrooms grow, and pour in fungicide. Treating the areas with magnesium sulphate (epsom salts), 2 tablespoons (40 ml) per gallon (4 liters) of water to every 2 square yards (1.7 square meters) of area, will also be very effective. If you only have a few mushrooms, pick them before the cap opens and spreads the spores. Put the mushrooms in a closed bag and dispose in the garbage or burn.

And now for my cherry tree. As usual, I had a fair crop of fruit, but now the rain has split most of it and the birds have taken care of the rest. I noticed a gum (pitch) coming out on one of the main branches. This is a disease called gumbosis and can only be cured through surgery. I'll take a sharp knife, cut out the gum until the wood is white and clear, wipe with a cloth dipped in bleach, and replace the cut out bark and wood with a tree emulsion. I'll do it all at once, and the branch will be restored to health. If I wait, the branch will die and the disease will spread through the tree.

The wonder plant was a favorite of Marco Polo

Often this time of year you will find garden centers featuring the aloe vera plants. I truly appreciate this very historical and much talked about specimen of the plant world. I wonder at its medicinal marvels, though I don't wish to express or imply any proof or real evidence with respect to its fitness for any particular purpose or use.

Nevertheless, I, too, have rubbed a festering wound, a scratch, or burn with the gel of the aloe vera and experienced fast healing.

I also know of people who are balding and now rubbing their heads with the same gel and are convinced they're growing hair again, and, similarly, I know of others drinking the gel for internal problems. It seems the whole world has suddenly discovered aloe vera as the medicine or wonder plant.

Aloe vera has become big business, especially with the various organizations in the skin care business. Whatever knowledge we have or whatever our personal experiences with the use of aloe vera, there is one thing certain: with all the interest and with all the experimentation presently taking place, we'll learn much more in the next several years about the merits of a plant used by people over the centuries.

For over 3500 years, tales of aloe vera healing have been handed down by word of mouth. From the Bible's mention of removing Christ from the cross and wrapping his body in aloes and myrrh, we find aloe vera mysteriously appearing in every phase of history, with many testimonials to its great medicinal values.

Legend tells us it was Cleopatra's beauty secret; it is believed the Egyptians used it, not just for beauty, but for embalming. We know Marco Polo found the Orientals using it for all things. Modern research has discovered substantial proof as to the powers of the gel contained in this age-old natural plant.

The effectiveness of aloe vera as a beauty treatment for velvety skin and lustrous, gleaming hair was so remarkable that some ancient maidens claimed it was a gift from Venus, the Goddess of Love.

The aloe is considered by many to be a member of the cactus family, but in reality it belongs to the lily family. There are over 200 species of the aloe plant but only one true aloe vera.

Aloe vera is not only valuable for medicinal purposes but is also attractive as a houseplant.

An ironic rediscovery of aloe vera

The aloe vera was only recently rediscovered. Ironically, it was the invention of the X-ray and the atom bomb which again focused attention upon the plant, for it was found early in the search for protection against radiation burns that the best treatment was aloe vera gel. As chemical, medical, and physical scientific research has progressed, many old remedies have been found to be worthless because they were based on faulty information and reasoning. Some, however, have been rediscovered to be infinitely superior to many synthetics. Aloe vera is one of the old natural remedies that has made an amazing comeback.

Aloe vera gel is an amazing mixture of natural antibiotic, astringent coagulating agent, a pain inhibitor, and a growth stimulator. Research has shown that the gel from the aloe vera leaf is capable of penetrating to the water-retaining second layer of skin, helping to stuff the dead cells gathered there and dissolving the root of infection. The plant itself provides much of the proof in this regard. The leaves have no stalk or woody parts and are kept upright by the water pressure of the gel.

Claims of aloe's cures are phenomenal

Today, the aloe plant is used by many people in many countries who maintain that it is nature's cure-all remedy for an unending list of ails. Undoubtedly there is an explanation. The juice of this plant is often added to drinks in cases of congestion and to prevent and counteract colic. It is also used to help purify water, since its chemical properties remove chlorine or fluoridation taste. The leaves of the plant are sometimes used for the treatment of infections of the skin, contusions, rheumatism, arthritis, and aching joints. It is said the pulp is used in the treatment of tumors, ulcers, open sores, ringworms, boils, acne, allergy rashes, psoriasis, itchings, burns and scalds, insect stings, and poison ivy. The gel of the aloe vera, when blended with milk and papaya, is believed to help kidney infections, sluggish livers, dysentery, stomach ulcers, and colitis.

158

Much of what I've heard about aloe vera is from the varied material that has come to me since I started to take greater interest, and my long-held curiosity for this interesting plant has been fed new hopes for much more potential. I do want to quickly disclaim having any medical evidence for aloe vera's properties, however.

Simple to grow, simple to use

To obtain the clear gel from the aloe vera is a very simple process. You need only to split a leaf and peel back the skin. The gel will then be immediately visible and ready for use. When filleting a mature leaf, the edges are removed to prevent cutting into the outer part of the leaf which has tubes filled with a bitter yellow juice. A dull knife is used to remove the outer skin of the broad side of the leaf to avoid cutting into the bitter tubes. The entire center of the leaf is full of clear gel.

Many feel that the quickest way to obtain relief from discomfort caused by burns, scalds, or open wounds is to bandage the split leaft itself to the affected area.

For internal consumption, the gel can be placed in some water in the refrigerator and then taken in teaspoon quantities or mixed with fruit drinks or other flavors.

Aloe vera is not only grown for its wonder herb but also because it is a hardy, ornamental, and virtually pest-free plant. You will often come across it in public buildings and gardens because of its stiff, rugged habit.

Although aloe vera is a native to the tropics, it can be grown in colder climates by treating it as tender pot plant. It likes rich soil, partial shade, and adequate, but not excessive water in soil with good drainage. Standing water around the roots must be avoided at all costs since it will rot the plant. Water the plant only when dry, usually once a week in summer and every ten days in winter, although much will depend on the room temperature, humidity, and size of pot.

The color of flowers vary, depending on the species of the aloe vera. Most, however, are orange and others cream-colored. Some species develop flowers as early as 10 months, while others will produce flowers only when the plant has reached maturity in 3 years.

July is the month gardens need tender loving care

This is the time of year when garden troubles begin to occur. The nature of the garden is important here. Some hardy tree shrubs, perennials, and even annuals may remain trouble-free all of their lives, yet a loved and cherished bush that has been with you for a long time could well be the host to an assortment of pests and diseases every season.

The weather is another basic factor; there will be slugs when it's wet, greenfly or aphids when it's dry, and red spider when it's hot.

We can all expect troubles, whether we're amateurs or experts. The big difference, of course, is that the expert knows what to look for, takes steps to cut down on the likelihood of pests and disease attack, and tackles the trouble as soon as it appears. We can all become expert, to varying degrees, of course, but learn we can and learn we should.

Garden troubles are tackled in two basic ways—culturally and chemically. Generally, both have a job to do in a well-tended garden. My motto is "an ounce of prevention is worth a pound of cure," and of all places to practice prevention, the garden ranks at the top of the list.

A well-prepared, properly drained soil grows healthier plants, much more able to withstand bugs and disease.

Keep the ground free from soil pests. Many insects live in the soil. Not all of them, however, are harmful to plants. Some are actually beneficial because they feed on garden pests. A rough guide to follow when digging and discovering unfamiliar bugs and grubs is if you can't catch it easily, kill it.

Too few of us realize the full value of feeding. A shortage of nutrients can lead to disease or disease-like symptoms, and certain bugs will attack the weakened and underfed plant. Especially after the many rains, the vegetable and flower garden should be fed a well-balanced fertilizer, such as Feed-All (7-7-7), and the lawn deserves the best Lawn Treat (13-5-7), Lawn Builder (10-6-4), or a fertilizer with a similar analysis.

Never leave rubbish lying about. Old plants, grass clippings, and boxes are a breeding ground for disease, slugs, woodlice, millipedes, wireworms, and cutworms. Burn woody and diseased material, and compost the rest.

Fertilizers keep quality up, prices down

Despite the rising cost of living, we in North America enjoy relatively low food costs. I'm not suggesting food is cheap, I'm merely pointing out that we have bountiful crops, enjoy varied diets from our own produce, and have more money left over for other things we need and want.

Obviously we have little control over such imported food products as pineapple, oranges, bananas, spices, coffee, or cane sugar, but where we really gain is through locally-grown fruits and produce, milk, and other dairy products.

You may wonder how, in times of continuing high inflation, we've managed to remain very competitive in food production. Some of the answers are pretty evident, not the least of which is mechanization and better land utilization.

Land prices have risen dramatically. The farm, which only a decade ago could be profitable without utilizing all the soil, is a thing of the past. Today, acreage is so expensive that every square foot counts.

The greatest impact on better land utilization has come from a greater use of fertilizers. Too few people realize the full value of proper plant feeding. We have to eat to live, and without a regular supply of starch, protein, and minerals, we too would very soon become ill or die. Our plants have more natural means. As long as certain simple chemicals are accessible to the roots, plants are able to make their own starch, protein, and other life-sustaining needs.

Soils have a built-in stock of plant foods, which come from the mineral part of the soil, from the humus the soil provides, and certain plants, which take elements or nutrients from the air and feed them back into the soil for the other plants to survive on. When soil is cultivated for intensive production of specific crops, the essential foods tend to diminish more rapidly than they can be replaced by natural means.

Three basic chemicals are often in short supply: nitrogen, phosphates, and potash. These are called the major plant foods.

Nitrogen is the leaf maker. It is essential for leafy vegetables and grass. The sign of shortage is a stunted plant with small, pale green leaves, and the solution is a compound fertilizer high in nitrogen. Numbers are used on the packages to show the strength of the fertilizer. For example, 13-5-7 has 13 percent nitrogen, 5 percent phosphate, and 7 percent potash. It must also be noted that the better fertilizers may contain more than one source of nitrogen or other elements, thus offering release over a longer period of time.

Phosphate is the root maker. Root crops are usually in need of this element. The sign of shortage is stunted plants with poorly developed roots. Again, a compound fertilizer is required or, alternatively, if no other elements are needed, a straight superphosphate which is 18 percent pure, or Bonemeal, a slow-acting fertilizer containing 30 percent pure phosphate, will do the job.

Potash is the flower and fruit maker. It is very necessary for flowering plants and fruit-producing trees, bushes, or vegatables. The signs of shortage are scorching of the leaves at the edges, poor coloration, and lack of flavor in fruits and vegetables. Use a compound fertilizer high in potash like 4-10-10, sulphate of potash, or wood ashes.

Plants may also require moderate amounts of calcium derived from lime or magnesium. Magnesium is especially useful for roses and tomatoes. A shortage of magnesium can be detected when pale or yellow areas develop between the veins on the leaves.

Remember, only minute amounts of trace elements may be needed for healthiest plant growth. Make sure that you use amounts as recommended on the package. Doubling the amount does not give twice the benefit.

Want privacy? Hedges beat costly fences

Much of the value in our home is determined by the amount of privacy it provides. Busy people, both Dad and Mom, who work and want a break from it all when they get back to the homestead, seek all the privacy they can get. The automobile, people on the move, as well as strangers on the prowl, make it even more important. Urban living and smaller lots are making it ever more difficult.

The trend has been to use screens or hedges. By far the most popular screen, for a variety of reasons, is the thuya, better known as Western red cedar. The most popular of the cedars are The *Thuya plicata,* which grows fast, tall, and broad. Even more popular are the different types of pyramidal cedar (*Thuya pyramidalis*), which grow slender, compact, neat, and narrow. Cedars have rapidly replaced the many cypress varieties because they're not subject to root rot, and the laurel because they're much hardier and keep their color even in the coldest winter.

A hedge is cheaper than a fence and much more permanent. The initial cost is less, and they require little upkeep. The cost per foot will depend upon the size of shrub with which you start, but since they're planted 30 to 36 inches (76 to 91 centimeters) apart and they grow relatively fast, even an inexpensive nonpermanent wooden screen will cost more initially and a lot more in the long run.

Screens or hedges are especially useful when you find it necessary to screen a dog pen or children's play area, control dust, or muffle street noise.

Climbing vines can help

Screens or hedges don't suit all people. Many enjoy the neighborhood activity and want to know all that's happening on their street. On smaller lots and with condominiums, there may

163

Lillian with an exotic climbing bougainvillea vine. This vine is not winter hardy but can be container grown on a patio.

not be enough room for hedges, and there are always those who say, "let the sun shine in." These are the people who can still break the hard lines and add a touch of privacy so absolutely necessary especially in the instant subdivisions, and for them I recommend the versatility and beauty of the climbing vines.

Vines and ivies are not intended to shut others out or us in, but instead they provide a special touch that sets your house apart from the rest, and makes a house a home. These climbing beauties can also be used to cover up an object that might detract from the overall beauty of your garden.

When you select a vine for flowers or foliage, or both, it should serve some special purpose. The vine can be used to cover an

PRIVACY AND VISUAL INTEREST.

objectionable surface, in which case you would most likely select a rather dense and fast growing climber of the evergreen species, such as ivy.

If the object or wall is concrete and there's no means of support, you would naturally select a self-clinging vine, such as a Boston ivy or Virginia creeper. When I wanted to cover an unsightly telephone pole on my property in one season, I chose the tremendously fast-climbing silver lace, which reached 25 feet (8 meters) in the first year. For the clothesline pole, I chose another similar fast-growing climber, wisteria, but what a mistake that was. It climbed up the pole and back along the clothesline before I knew what happened.

Firethorn a best seller

For the smaller garden, I recommend the climbing rose, the fragrant honeysuckle, or the princess of the garden, clematis. Lately, it seems the favorite best seller, however, is the pyracantha, commonly called firethorn. It is evergreen, blooms in spring, and produces and enormous mass of orange-red berries that grace the garden all winter long.

For the backyard, try the fruiting vines. A sunny spot, especially against the south wall, can produce enough grapes for the fall table as well as a stock of jelly and a few gallons of wine. That low fence around the vegetable patch is excellent for an evergreen blackberry or the old-fashioned boysenberry and loganberry vines, giving still more jam, jelly, or homemade wine.

Q: **What's the basic rule for growing clematis?**
A: Clematis like well-drained, sweet soil, with roots in the shade and tops in the sun.

Q: **What do you feed your vines?**
A: If the vine flowers, I use garden food, and if it's all foliage, I

use lawn food.

Q: When do I transplant German iris or flags?
A: Now—midsummer. Dig up, divide, and cut back foliage to 6 inches (15 centimeters) above tuber cutting—not straight across, but in an upright V—and transplant to new location in fertile ground, covering tuber with only a few inches of soil.

Q: How do I kill earwigs without using an insecticide?
A: Roll up a wet newspaper and leave between your plants during the night. The earwigs crawl in at night and you can burn it the next morning.

Q: For the second year in a row my pyracantha lacks bloom. How can I make it have it more berries?
A: Feed it a low-nitrogen fertilizer and screen it from drying winds while it is flowering.

Q: Are coffee grounds good for evergreens?
A: Three cups of coffee grounds a season are recommended for rhododendrons, azaleas, and other broadleaf evergreens.

Q: My lawn has some soggy spots caused by water damage. Will it pick up?
A: Not without some help. Cut through the soggy spots on three sides of the sod and gently roll back the sod and fill it with top soil. Press this down firmly and then roll back the sod to its original place and press it firmly to the new soil.

August

Ground covers can grow under tough conditions

One of the greatest plant time savers, although not as well known as they should be, are the ground covers. Anyone who attempts to grow grass under trees or in heavily shaded areas is fighting a losing battle. It will only be a matter of time before you're back to bare soil or weeds.

Ground covers are the answer to your prayers and will save you many headaches. These tough boys can take on almost any situation: shade, part shade, dampness, or spongy soil. Put the right variety in the right place and you can actually see them grow.

To help your ground covers get started, spade in plenty of peat moss or old manure and add some bonemeal or organic fertilizer. The soil should be prepared just as if you were planting a flower or vegetable garden, and it should be level and fine. I can't wait too long for the results, so I place the plants much closer together in staggered rows. I feed the plants a regular lawn food twice a year.

Ground covers can be planted almost year round, provided there's a plentiful water supply available. Personally, however, I prefer to plant in April and May.

There are others who appreciate the beauty of the ground cover. Many bugs could invade the area, and mice or moles will build a winter home beneath the shelter and protection of a thick, dense cover. To discourage the insects, spray with any recommended insecticide. As I stated in the June chapter, bury a wine bottle or two spout up so the wind will blow in, and the noise will keep the moles moving.

Watch ground covers choke out weeds

Weeds are little, if any, problem. Once the ground covers fill in,

170

there's just no room for weeds. I have a beautiful, long bed of zabel laurel ground cover along my driveway, and when it was first planted, I raked between it in early spring and applied a weed preventer. I've never had weeds in the bed since.

You may wonder how I can classify zabel laurel (which in the last few years has grown 6 feet across and 6 feet high (1.8 x 1.8 meters) as a ground cover, but it does in fact solidly cover the ground and makes a beautiful showing.

Ground covers are more than just decorative. It is true that they are most attractive in places where grass won't grow: under trees, on a steep bank that can't be mowed, between two walls in a very shady area, or in areas along walkways or driveways where regular mowing is just too difficult. It is also true that some ground covers will grow where it is too wet for grass to survive, and still others will grow where it is too dry.

Ground covers will cool the soil around your favorite tree, but most important of all, ground covers prevent soil erosion and will hold banks, slopes, and hills in place perfectly, thus preventing erosion, which potentially could involve huge losses of property and property values.

Ground covers are most useful in smaller areas where the gardener wants a lawnlike appearance with a minimum of work, no mowing, little watering, and only an occasional feeding. You should consider arenaria or Irish moss or several of the excellent thymes, such as the creeping or woolly varieties. Planted in a staggered fashion about 1 foot (30 centimeters) apart, they'll soon provide a solid cover.

There are also those ground covers which are excellent for filling between rose bushes or other flowering shrubs: carpet bugle (*ajuga*), Aaron's beard (*hypericum*), rock rose (*gaultheria*), sedum, snow-in-summer (*cerastium*), creeping achillea, and others.

Between rocks or in places difficult to reach, try cotoneaster, heather, mahonia, rosemary, or ceanothus. Along that walkway or on the steep banks, cotoneaster, ivy, periwinkle, or pachysandra will be just great.

Bill and friend Marchella Carniel check homegrown grapes in a backyard with southern exposure.

Many varieties of grapes suitable for desserts and wines are now available in the Pacific northwest.

Utilize everything from your garden, even for wine

Being of Dutch heritage and having gone through World War II, when everything was put to good use with absolutely no waste, I'm becoming increasingly interested in utilizing everything from the garden.

Put everything to good use; if you have an abundance and find you have more than you can eat, preserve the food by canning, drying, or freezing. You can also brew it, and come up with some of the best wines in North America.

I'm not a beer drinker, so when the various brewery strikes run on and prices increase, it matters little to me. But it matters to many. And many consider the alternatives. Why not consider mastering the art of wine making, using the bounty from your yard and garden?

The vegetables, fruit, and flowers from which wine can be produced are almost endless. Recipe sheets are available at the better garden centers everywhere.

Lillian's apple-cranberry wine

First week:
   6 lbs. (3 kg) apples (any tart variety)
   8 cups (1.5 kg) cranberries
   4 quarts (4 liters) water
Second Week:
   8 cups (1.5 kg) cane sugar
   1 slice of toast
   1 oz. (30 g) wet yeast
   2 cups (0.5 kg) muscal raisins

Chop the cranberries very fine and place them in a canning pot. Pour 2 quarts (2 liters) of boiling water over them. This will set the red color of the wine. Set aside to cool. Chop the apples very fine and add to

174

the cranberries along with the remaining two quarts (2 liters) of water.

Cover and put in a warm place to ferment for one week. Then strain through a jelly bag, squeezing very dry. Return to the canning pot and add sugar; stir well so that all sugar is dissolved. Add the chopped raisins.

Moisten the yeast with a few drops of water and spread on one side of the toast. Float the toast, yeast side down on the surface of the liquid. Set in a warm place to ferment for 2 more weeks. Stir twice a week.

At the end of this 2 week period, strain again through the jelly bag, squeezing it dry, and return to the canning kettle to settle 2 days longer.

Now siphon off into clean, sterilized bottles and cork lightly until fermentation ceases. After the wine has stopped all activity, cork tightly and seal with paraffin. Keep for at least 4 months before drinking.

Bill's beet wine

10 lbs. (4.5 kg) beets
1 lb (0.5 kg) raisins
3 cut-up lemons
8 lbs (3.5 kg) sugar
1 pkg. powdered yeast

Boil beets until tender. Add water to beet juice to make 2 gallons (8 liters) of liquid. Add above ingredients.

To fix yeast:
½ cup (125 ml) lukewarm water
1 tsp. (5 ml) white sugar

Mix sugar and water. Stir. Pour powdered yeast on top. Let stand for 10 minutes. Pour yeast mixture over top of beet juice. Let stand 2 weeks, then strain and bottle.

(Note: Turnips or carrots may be substituted for beets in this recipe).

Potato champagne

 7 potatoes
 7 oranges
 7 lemons
 7 lbs. (3.5 kg) of sugar
 7 quarts (7 liters) of water
 1 lb. (0.5 kg) raisins (ground)
 1 pkg. dry yeast
 1 slice toast

Peel and slice oranges, lemons, and potatos. Place in a crock and add the rest of the ingredients. Mix well with a wooden spoon. Place yeast on toast in water, yeast side down and remove in 1 week. Let the mixture sit; strain in 2 weeks, then strain again in 3 days. Then let the mixture sit 3 days, strain, and bottle.

Fraser Valley blossom wine

 1 quart (1 liter) dandelion blossoms
 4 quarts (4 liters) water
 ½ cup (125 ml) tepid water
 1 yeast cake
 1 lb. (0.5 kg) seedless raisins
 3 lbs. (1.5 kg) sugar
 1 lemon
 1 orange

Measure a generous quart (liter) of the dandelion blossoms, but do not use any of the stems. Put them into a large saucepan with the water and boil for 30 minutes.

Pour through a strainer, then strain through cheese-cloth into a large stone jar. When cool, add the yeast cake dissolved in the tepid water, raisins, sugar, lemon, and orange cut into small pieces, including the skins.

Stir every day for 2 weeks, then strain and let stand for a day to settle. Now strain carefully through cheese-cloth until clear. Bottle and seal.

(This recipe can also be made with roses, violets, clover flowers, or any other sweet blossoms.)

You owe it to yourself and the birds to plant berries

It really doesn't matter where you go or how far you travel, how luscious they appear on the shelf, or how well they may be served in the fanciest restaurant, you will never taste better berries than those picked directly from your own berry patch.

They take only a few feet of space so there's always somewhere for a few strawberry plants, raspberry, blueberry, gooseberry, or boysenberry bushes. You owe it to yourself, your garden, and the birds to plant at least a small berry patch. You'll treasure it always.

Strawberries are about the easiest crop to grow. A well prepared, good soil, full sunlight, and some tender loving care will provide you with unbelievable returns in delightful eating and plenty of satisfaction.

The berries are the heavy feeders in the garden. They like rich food and plenty of it, and they prefer an acid soil. To prepare the bed, apply a liberal quantity of cow or horse manure, 50 pounds (23 kilograms) per 10 square yards (8 square meters). If preparing the planting area in the fall, work in an equal amount of compost, plus 3 pounds (1.4 kilograms) of 13-5-7 or similarly numbered fertilizer. Spade under and allow to sit over winter, but spread

177

over the top about 10 pounds (4.5 kilograms) of gray lime to every 10 square feet (8 square meters). When spring comes, spade the bed again and level to a grade which will allow a slight crown for drainage.

Do not feed your berry plants before or after fruiting in the spring, as this will cause excess plant growth and reduce fruit production or cause poor quality fruit. The best time to plant in our area would be in the months of April and May, but I gave you so many chores to do in April, that I thought after a summer of having berry treats I could more easily convince you to put one or more varieties on your list for next year's planting.

One of the most important things to remember when planting berry bushes is that the plants should be set at the right depth. If plants are too deep or too shallow, they will die.

Strawberries   Plant so that the crown is just at soil level. If planted too shallow, the roots will dry out. If planted too deeply, they will rot.

Raspberries   Plant 3 inches (7 centimeters) deeper than they were grown. Cut the tops back to 12 inches (30 centimeters) and place the plants about 18 inches (46 centimeters) apart in the rows.

Blackberries   Follow the same procedure outlined for raspberries.

Currants and gooseberries   Plant 2-year-old plants. Place them 3 feet (90 centimeters) apart. Cut tops back to 8 inches (20 centimeters). Set plants 1 inch (2.5 centimeters) deeper than they previously were planted.

Grapes   Plant 1- or 2-year-old vines, 6 feet (1.8 meters) apart, and 2 inches (5 centimeters) deeper than they were in the nursery. Prune grapes in the dead of winter, leaving only pencil-sized canes.

Strawberries should be given a feeding of 13-5-7 or similarly numbered fertilizer during late August or early September. These plants make fruit buds in the fall for next year's crop. Grapes are fed just as they begin to grow, using a 2-14-6 or similarly numbered fertilizer. This same procedure is used for the other bush crops as well.

Keep your berry plants and bushes free from weeds since weeds steal valuable plant food, harbor bugs, and spread disease.

Refer to the April chapter for specifics on pruning berry bushes.

Ecology begins at home

If we all took pollution control seriously and practiced it in our every day lives, pollution could soon be a thing of the past.

For starters, don't burn leaves or grass clippings. They make a great supply of compost. The savings in your compost box or pile can be worked back into the soil come fall or spring.

Why use plastics under your mulches? Plastic will not decompose and return to the soil. Instead, try 3 or 4 layers of newspapers under the mulch, wood chips, or bark. Minimize (preferably eliminate) the use of pesticides.

However, until you get a reasonably good system that works for you, it may be necessary to depend on the least damaging. Use a liquid, selective weedkiller applied directly to the weeds instead of spreading a weed-and-feed over the entire lawn area whether it needs it or not.

Instead of spraying your rose bushes each week with a contact insecticide, which kills not only the bad bugs but also the good bugs, try a paint-on systemic. A nursery can best advise you on these improved approaches to eliminating the pests in your garden but, better still, try the organic and ecological approaches. A well-kept lawn will not encourage weeds; practice companion planting in your vegetable garden, and try the new organic bug killers like insecticidal soap.

Q: How do I make my poinsettia from last year bloom again?
A: From the end of September, careful light control is essential.

Cover with a black polyethelene bag from early evening and remove next morning so that the plant is kept in total darkness for 14 hours. Continue daily for 8 weeks; then treat normally.

Q: When and how do we prune our boysenberries?
A: Start now, in August, by cutting out the old canes that had fruit completely to the ground. Train remaining canes, but prune back to 6 feet (2 meters). These canes will develop side branches in the remainder of the growing season, and these should be cut back to 12 inches (30 centimeters) in early spring. With new spring growth, small branches grow from the side branches. These will carry the fruit.

Q: Can you give me the name of a fragrant ground cover?
A: Try peppermint, but let your "smeller" make your decision.

Q: Can I plant ground cover through plastic for weed control?
A: Sure you can—but I don't advise it. Plastic can be a pain in the you-know-what when it begins to tear with age. Mulch and weed preventers are much more serviceable.

Q: How often do you trim ground cover?
A: Whenever they get out of hand. Leave them only where you actually want them.

September

Collect and grow your own seeds

You are bound to have your failures with your successes, but through trial and error, and persistence, you will get addicted to what will be fun and challenging.

You may want to collect seeds from your favorite annuals or perennials and, perhaps, shrubs. Collect them in your own garden or from a friend, or pick from that beautiful specimen in the park. No one should mind; it won't hurt the plant.

Don't be too ambitious at first by collecting something of everything, but instead concentrate on several items to begin with.

When you collect, be sure to label so that you know what you are seeding when the appropriate time arrives.

All plants, trees, shrubs, or flowers contain both male and female parts. The male fertilizes the female part with the help of wind, bees, flies, or other insects. Once this sexual exercise is complete the flower fades and develops the embryo surrounding the seed. The embryo grows, developing necessary nutrients, normally carbohydrates, that are stored to nourish the seed during dormancy and to provide the initial food to make it grow into an infant plant.

The embryo usually has a good protective coating which will prevent it from damage and help contain the nutrients, and only when the protective coating is penetrated with moisture at the appropriate time and mixed with oxygen does the growth inside begin to take place. If seeds are stored too long, the seed will consume the embryo and growth will not take place. Seeds can normally be stored two to three years, although this period of possible storage is reduced when the embryo contains fatty substances.

Some seeds are sown green; for example, snow drops. Most seeds, however, need to ripen and require a period of cooling during dormancy before they will properly germinate. The best time to collect seeds is just as they have ripened but before they fall, although for some trees whose seeds are hard, the seed is better picked slightly green and stored in a refrigerator for planting the following spring.

The reason for picking slightly green is that if, with certain trees, the embryo develops too hard a casing, germination may not come easily, while if picked before that casing is fully developed and the seed kept cool, the nutrient in the embryo is there without the hard casing.

Bigger seeds germinate more easily than small seeds, which is why most plants producing small seeds do so in very large quantities. The smaller seeds do not store as much of the nutrient and thus will not germinate as readily.

Seeds collected from your flowers in the garden may not grow since while seed collected commercially is line bred and generally grown in isolation, the seed collected by you may have been pollinated by chance, involving a strange partner of the same species.

Seeds surrounded by fruit should be broken open and the seeds dried in trays with plenty of bottom air circulation. The seeds collected from flower-heads should be hung to dry with the heads in a paper bag loosely tied around the stems. Shake the bag every now and again so that the seeds fall to the bottom. Once the seed is dry it should be cleaned and stored in a cool, dry place, or, as mentioned earlier, in a refrigerator.

The very hard seeds such as those of the lupine may need to be scored with a razor blade or scratched on some sandpaper before seeding. This procedure will allow the moisture to penetrate more easily and mix with the oxygen to induce growth.

The rule of thumb has us seeding the trees, shrubs, and annuals in early spring, and perennials in early summer. Usually, the seeds are started indoors where conditions can be better controlled.

For seeding, best results are obtained with a light, sandy compost commercially available as starter mix. The soil should be placed in flats or pots and firmed, but not compacted. The seeds should be covered with sufficient compost to equal the approximate thickness of the seed.

The pot, box, or flat should be moistened or watered by standing it in a shallow bath so that the water moves upward by capilliary action. The container should be covered with a piece of glass and placed in a warm, dark place, or you may cover the glass with a sheet of paper.

I mentioned earlier that it takes water and oxygen to make the seed grow. Thus it is important that you do not use heavy or soggy soil through which oxygen cannot penetrate. The seeds should be sown carefully so they are not too thick in the box or pot.

As soon as the seeds begin to appear penetrating the soil surface, remove the paper or move the flats to a little more light. Be careful to move it to light gradually, as otherwise the seedlings will burn.

There's a lot of truth in old wives' tales

A long-time Surrey friend, and possibly one of the finest and most understanding of Crescent Beach gardeners, is Honey (Marie) Hooser. Honey is over 80, but acts no older than she did 40 years ago.

Honey is a great gardener and has a real knowledge and feel for the garden, but, best of all, she is a collector of the unusual. Honey's garden is where you find and learn about the rare alpines and rockery plants, the varieties of rockery cyclamen, the gentians, the primulas.

Honey recently filled me in on a lot of gardening nuggets and old wives' tales. Honey, like myself, believes that it's good to sprinkle some superstition with a lot of good sense.

Every old wives' tale will tell you to sow seed and to transplant only with a waxing, never a waning, moon. Science has now discovered the effects of lunar rhythms on the earth's magnetic field, which, in turn, affect growth. Scientists have established that all water everywhere, including that inside the tiniest living organism, moves in tides like the sea. The moon also affects the earth's atmoshpere so that statistically it is more likely to rain heavily (just what you need immediately after planting) following a full or new moon. Honey tells me that a potato grown at constant levels of heat and light under laboratory conditions will still show a growth rhythm that reflects the lunar pattern. The scientists learn through their experiments and with the aid of expensive equipment, but the old wives learned from experience.

Many decades back it was believed that the greatest success from planting or seeding the garden was obtained when planting was done in the nude.

Superstition or magic? Maybe not.

We all know that we should not sow the garden when the ground is too cold, and we're less likely to do so we must undertake the task while naked.

An old wife tells us that we should put hair in the bottom of a trench when planting beans. The barber of old saved all the hair from his shop and had a lovely bean crop; and some gardeners used horsehair, believing the sharpness would prick the bugs to death. They believed it worked. Scientists now know that hair contains many trace elements beneficial to plants and not otherwise available in soil or normal plant nutrients.

They used to plant strawberries during the waxing moon (in the nude) with plenty of pine and fir needles in the belief that this gave the strawberries better flavor. We now know that pine and fir needles cause acidity, and acid soil makes strawberries more flavorful.

When for some reason it is necessary to transplant at a time of year when it is too cold, puddle the plants in, using hot water instead of cold. Surprisingly enough, this really does not damage the roots.

The French use marigolds more than anyone. In France nearly every garden, whether it displays flowers or vegetables, boasts a marigold edging. Both the aroma and the root excretions are invaluable. The French were aware that marigolds killed nematodes and white fly and were especially valuable to potatoes and tomatoes. It has now been found that the African tagetes variety is even more effective.

Perhaps the best old wives' tale is one that I intend to try personally. They say that Mexican tagetes will control ground ivy and horsetail. I have a bank of horsetail, and I've tried everything else, so next year you'll see the most colorful bank of marigolds to be seen anywhere.

Speaking of horsetail, in the old days it was regularly used for scouring pewter dishes and wooden implements. It still works better for aluminum saucepans than almost anything else.

Banana skins laid just below the surface of the soil have long been said to be very good for roses, and the experts now approve the practice. They have found that banana peels rot very quickly and provide a considerable quantity of calcium, magnesium, sulphur, phosphates, sodium, and silica.

Don't throw away your old egg cartons. They work like peat pots for growing small seedlings.

Keep old nylons; there really is nothing better for tying trees.

I used to have to get up in the very early morning to spray the tender bedding plants when we had frost during the night. If you spray with water before the sun rises, even the tenderest of plants when frozen, you won't lose them. I've now learned, too late, that if they are sprayed with cold water in the evening, the evaporation of the water during the night will give off sufficient heat to prevent frost damage.

More odd-ball practices

Actually, one can learn much from the practices of days gone by and, for the most part, long forgotten.

The old wives' tales are endless, but I've selected a few more that are reasonably practical. Don't knock them until you've tried them.

Remember seeing that horse head carved in stone above the old garden gate? This was a relic from Roman times. Displaying the stone carving was considered to make the garden more fruitful.

Gardeners in England, when digging deep, will often turn up very old earthen pots. These were used to bury toads, believed to offer protection against storms and hail.

The Germans used to hang a jar with a little beer in the fruit trees or amongst the bushes in the fall to attract wasps and let them commit suicide at their leisure.

Before the various poisonous slug baits became so popular, one of the methods of elimination was to place beer in a dish to attract them. Yet another was bran or orange peel on the ground covered with a pinned down cabbage leaf; then in the morning, the colony of slugs could be sprinkled with salt or lime.

To prevent mice from feasting on newly sown peas, the Welsh used to put holly clippings in the trenches, and they also poked bramble sticks down the mole runs, effectively moving the critters next door to their neighbors.

I used to keep a frog in my little greenhouse, supposedly for good luck, but it was a real pet and took care of many insects.

Prepare to give your plants a pleasant winter rest

By the end of September all the Holland bulbs will have arrived and the gardener's attention will naturally turn to planting those spring flowering beauties in bed or border, planter, or rockery.

The avid gardener will naturally grow some indoors for blooms on the kitchen table or on the front room windowsill at Christmas and throughout the months of January, February, and March. My favorites are the hyacinth, crocus, miniature tulip, regular tulip, and daffodil. More on this in the November chapter.

I'm worried about all those indoor plants on the patio. In mid-September I bring in the ferns from my front walkway. They provide a tremendous show amongst my fuchsias all summer, and they grow like you wouldn't believe. I'm worried that a lot of our friendly gardeners will leave them outside too long, and they'll become so exposed to the elements of fall weather that the transition to the home might prove fatal.

Dahlias are often at their best in late summer and fall.

You can help your plants weather the winter

Most houseplants are tropical or semitropical and require a humidity level of 30 to 40 percent. Your home may have a humidity level of only 10 percent or less when the outside temperature is low for any prolonged period of time. A humidifier is the ideal way to raise your home's humidity to the level plants need, but there are other steps you can take.

Incidentally, humidifiers are good for you, too; you'll feel better and have fewer colds.

Daily misting of your plants helps, but it's much more effective to mist several times per day, and that isn't always easy.

Try setting your plant pots on a wetted gravel bed in a saucer; the slowly evaporating water will create the necessary moisture. Try surrounding the plant pots with moist sphagnum moss by placing the plant pot inside a jardiniere and filling the space between the pot and jardiniere with the moss. This is effective and simple.

Check the plants you have summered outdoors for any signs of pests. The last thing you need over the winter is a bout of bugs.

Remember, south sun is much stronger now and north light much weaker, so move your plants to positions where they can get proper light. Be careful not to put sun sensitive plants too close to south windows, and be certain the plants in north windows can exist with minimum light. Check plants regularly for water, but, remember, plants need much less watering in winter than summer. Cactus and succulents go partially dormant and can stand going very dry between waterings.

Stop fertilizing your blooming plants and others that need a winter rest period. Your ferns and foliage plants can also get by with less fertilizer.

Move all your plants away from heat registers. The hot, dry air can have a sudden and disastrous effect on your plants.

Dust plants with a soft moistened cloth when dust builds up. Wipe only the top sides of the leaves (the pores the plant breathes through are located on the underside of the leaves). Wipe gently so you don't damage tender plant cells.

You may use a plant shine to make the leaves sparkle but don't overdo it as this can cause a build-up.

To water your hanging baskets properly, take them off their hooks and place them in the sink so that they can be watered thoroughly and properly, and not simply teased till they die.

Watering in winter, by rule of thumb, should take place when the soil begins to dry. Water less often, and use tepid (not cold) water.

Learn about bulbs and then select for spring showing

To best learn about bulbs, you should probably become more familiar with what they are.

Plants that grow from bulbs, corms, or tubers have widely differing structures but are alike in possessing a fleshy organ from which roots are produced and in which food and water are stored.

Because of their capacity for storing food and water, plants grown from bulbs, corms, or tubers can normally do without water for long periods, even while growing actively. During the rest period, they generally become completely dormant.

Though bulbs, corms, or tubers all produce feeding roots, leaves, stems, and flowers, they differ in many ways.

A bulb, for instance, is a modified leaf brill. Bulbs and corms produce roots from the base only. Tubers can produce roots from the top and sides. The top growth of bulbs and corms is stemless, with leaves and flower stalks sprouting directly from the neck.

A hardy bulb can not only withstand frost but is ordinarily unable to survive unless planted outdoors after flowering in the home. Such plants as hyacinths, narcissuses, tulips, and crocuses belong to this group.

Plant now for spring

Planting time for spring flowering bulbs is September to December, with earlier planting preferable. Fall bulb planting most often occurs after the first frost when all the summer annuals have died.

Bulbs can be viewed as a plant family with enormous opportunity. They can be planted most anywhere, dug at the appropriate time, and shipped the world over.

Dutch bulbs thrive in sun or shade as long as the soil is well drained. Plant tulips, daffodils, hyacinths, and other large bulbs 6 inches deep and 6 inches apart (15 by 15 centimeters) in clusters of 20 or more of each variety. Smaller bulbs, such as crocus, scilla, mascari, and snowdrops, need to be planted only 3 inches deep and 3 inches apart (7 by 7 centimeters).

Give careful consideration to the flowering dates and height of growth so that you plant the groups in proper order.

If planting in a very clay-like soil, it may be necessary to add sand, peat, or perlite. Firmly but carefully set the bulb into the soil, pointed end up, and water liberally after replacing the soil in order to begin root formation vital for your spring flower environment.

Bulbs contain their own food supply, but fertilizer will foster future growth and make for bigger and continued bloom. The best fertilizer would be bonemeal or bulbfood placed under the bulb at time of planting.

Spring will be most rewarding and you'll love the beauty of the stately tulips. The joys of spring as seen in the daffodil and the fragrance of the hyacinth that scent the total garden are a small but important part of the coming of spring heightened by the popping of crocuses through the grass and in the rock garden.

The flowers are removed as they begin to wilt; otherwise the plant will go to seed carrying away nutrients needed for next season's growth. The greens are left to die down naturally before they're removed and the bulb remains to bloom again another year.

If you wish to move the bulbs to another spot in the garden, you may do so after the bulb tops have died down. Perhaps the bulbs after several years may have split and should be replanted.

In either case, allow the bulbs to dry in a spot that's cool and airy, though sheltered from the burning sun. Keep the bulbs out of the soil for a rest period until fall planting at which time a soil dust and plant food should be added.

Raising springtime tulips

For regal appearance, the tulip tops the list. I usually start setting out tulip bulbs in mid-September.

Tulips may be planted in any location, sun or shade, and they are usually planted about 6 inches (15 centimeters) deep and that distance apart. They can be planted with other types of bulbs that bloom about the same time or with winter pansies or wallflowers. Always be sure that the tulips remain the dominant feature. The tulip may be dropped in an individual hole, or you can dig out the entire planting area to the required depth, spread in the bulb food, set the bulbs in place, and cover the entire area with soil. This latter procedure is easiest for large planting areas and also assures that the bulbs will all flower at one time. Bulbs prefer a light, sandy, or loamy soil with good drainage.

The latest technique is to plant 3 or more bulbs in a container with good drainage holes, cover with a bit of gravel, and place these containers in a growing area. The growing area can be last summer's vegetable garden. Bury the pots to a depth of about 4 to 6 inches (10 to 15 centimeters), as the bulbs will only be planted a few inches deep in the pot. Or build yourself a raised bed 12 inches (30 centimeters) deep, putting the containers on the bottom and away from the sides of the bed. Then cover the whole thing in sawdust.

This method of growing allows you to lift the pots when and where the need arises, preferably when the bulbs are 4 inches (10 centimeters) out of the pot when taking them indoors or 6 inches (15 centimeters) out of the pot when using them to fill the bare spots in the garden. They can finish blooming, either in the house or where you buried them outside. You can move the containers back to the growing area to allow the tops to die slowly and naturally; this assures good, healthy bulbs for the following year.

192

We have many tulip classifications, allowing for blooms starting in March and lasting until June. When planting tulips, keep in mind the various classes. The most popular are easily divided into three basic categories—species or early flowering rockery tulips, early flowering dwarf tulips in either single or double flowers, and mid- and late-season flowering varieties, which include the tall, stately Darwin flowering varieties.

The species tulips are the earliest to bloom. They're generally very bright colored, short stemmed, and they seem to produce year after year with the least difficulty.

The next group are the double and single early tulips. They are short stemmed, very colorful in planters and borders, and bloom in April.

The Darwin type tulips (with this group I'm including the mendel,triumph, and cottage types) are longer stemmed, later blooming, longer lasting, and very showy. They are most popular outdoors but not as good indoors as the types mentioned earlier. The Darwin hybrid tulips have the biggest blooms, often up to 6 inches (15 centimeters) across when fully open and will stand on stems up to 28 inches (71 centimeters) high.

The lily-flowered tulips are extremely graceful. They have lovely pointed petals on wiry, strong stems, giving a great show starting late April.

The most exciting tulip is the exquisite parrot variety. These heavily frilled tulips are huge; they grow to 2 feet (60 centimeters) tall and bloom from May to June.

The tulip that looks like a peony and has flowers in all colors blooming in May or June, is the double late or peony flowered tulip.

Daffodils and narcissuses are fragrant and varied

Daffodils are among the easiest bulbous flowers. The daffodils can be planted individually or in groups in swales.

Daffodils are often wild, though they have been naturalized and are planted in groups under bushes or trees. The most popular daffodil is the yellow trumpet type, but greater variety and color combinations are in the large-cupped types. The latter vary from such combinations as yellow perianths with white cups to the reverse with red or orange cups, or shades of either, including pink.

The most fragrant narcissuses (also the botanical name for the daffodil), are the poetaz or cluster types. These are generally white, though they can also be found in yellow or combinations of white and yellow, and bloom long and faithfully year after year.

Plant your daffodils and narcissuses in a well drained, sandy loam soil. Add plenty of humus and bonemeal or bulb food if you want to enjoy blooms year after year.

Plant both daffodils and narcissuses 5 inches deep and 5 inches apart (13 by 13 centimeters). If you have an ample supply of bulbs, you may plant closer; it does make more of an impact. Plant in sun, shade, or partial shade.

There are different flowering times for continued bloom from the early species or rockery varieties, which start in January and February, to the big yellow daffodils in March and April, and the small-cupped narcissuses and doubles in May or June.

A few blooms of hyacinth scent an entire room

In the outdoor garden, hyacinths will produce a most interesting display. In groups of three or five bulbs, hyacinths can do more in a garden than any other bulb. In addition, they will appear most impressive in beds and borders; for a massed effect, you will also find them valuable in front of daffodils, early tulips, or in a mixed border.

Hyacinths should be planted in a rich, sandy soil. Space the bulbs 6 inches apart and 6 inches deep (15 by 15 centimeters), Hyacinths, like tulips and daffodils, may be planted in containers. There is a wide variety of hyacinths available in all shades of blue, red, pink, white, yellow, and orange. You might consider planting hyacinths to complement forget-me-nots. They make a terrific combination.

Hyacinths can also be grown indoors in ordinary gravel or in water by using a special hyacinth vase. Always use one variety and color per pot to have them all bloom at the same time.

In my garden, I have grape hyacinths planted throughout the bedding plants to provide a lovely show of profuse royal blue.

The grape hyacinths are deep enough that I can plant my annuals on top and they multiply and simply keep coming up with no care or attention. The longest lasting blooms in my garden are the variety blue spike. These are a beautiful Dutch blue miniature hyacinth-like flower that blooms in my borders from March to June.

Our faithful announcer of spring, the crocus

The most popular of the little bulbs is the crocus. These are the jewels of spring and often will appear above ground before the snow is gone. They are referred to as bulbs but are really corms and should be set in clumps or groups to provide a mass of color. Crocuses also do well in the lawn where regular mowing is not required. Merely cut through the sod and set the corms at a depth of 3 inches (7 centimeters). The color range includes shades of white, white with blue stripes, blue, violet, purple, and yellow.

There are two types of spring flowering crocus: the specie type and the regular type.

The specie type may bloom outdoors as early as Christmas in a protected area, and between January and February is quite normal. The regular crocus bloom in February and March.

The earliest signs of spring are the winter crocus, snowdrop, chionodoxa, and eranthis (winter aconite). Many a year these will pop through the ground right after Christmas.

There are many more beautiful flowering bulbs, not the least of which is the windflower (anemone).

195

Explore all the possibilities

Visiting your favorite garden center will give you an education in the many varieties and endless possibilities for bulbs.

Some of my favorites are the snowdrops which grow most anywhere—the lawn, rockery, or just on or near a tree stump. The snowdrop blooms in the middle of winter, even if there is snow on the ground.

Another is the scilla or squill, of which there are several types, though the dwarf winter blooming variety is more popular than the taller bluebell which blooms in May and June.

The poor man's orchid is the Dutch iris. Irises have lovely orchid-like blooms in May and June and are available in a range of blues, whites, and yellows, or combinations of these. They make excellent, long lasting cut flowers.

One of my favorite planting combinations are King Alfred daffodils in back, red emperor tulips in front, and grape hyacinths ahead of that.

It takes little effort this fall to have an enviable spring starting this winter.

Q: The leaves on my dogwood tree turned red prematurely and are now falling off. What's happening?
A: Your dogwood is drowning! Check for drainage quickly.

Q: I want a palm for my vestibule. Which variety do you recommend?
A: Try the neanthe bella palm. It's slower growing but stronger than most other varieties. Give it plenty of humidity but keep only evenly moist during winter.

Q: Why was I told to cut back almost half of my new tree when transplanting or planting bareroot?
A: The top is cut back to equalize the moisture loss as a result of root reduction.

196

October

Most plants need a break come winter

Most books on houseplant care usually give you the same list of essential needs—light, water, warmth, humidity, fertilizer—but one requirement is often overlooked: *a period for rest.*

Nearly all of our indoor plants need a dormant period during the year, and usually this takes place in winter. Some plants give clear signs that they are at the end of their growth period, and even a greenhorn can tell that the usual care and upkeep routine needs to change. The top growth of bulbous and tuberous plants (begonia, gloxinia or cyclamen), dies down; the leaves of deciduous woody plants, such as poinsettia, drop off. Watering is greatly reduced or stopped altogether. The resting period has come.

Evergreeen tropical plants, unfortunately, give little or no indication that a period of rest is needed. But as midwinter approaches, the duration of natural light is too short for active growth. It is necessary to reduce the frequency of watering and feeding; cooler conditions may be required. If the plant is kept warmer than recommended and watered as frequently as in spring, then it will definitely develop problems.

The first sign of new growth in the spring will be a sure sign that the resting period is over. Slowly begin normal watering and feeding, and repot the plant if needed. Some plants, such as African violets, seem to have little need of a resting period, but they do benefit from a period of about a month when watering and feeding are reduced to below normal.

There is an important exception to the need for a winter rest period. Winter-flowering pot plants must be fed and watered regularly for as long as they are on display indoors.

Your time for rest and relaxation away from home is a period of strain for the indoor plants which remain behind, but a little preparation before you leave will guarantee that they will not be too bothered by you being away.

That winter trip

Leaving plants for a week or two during the winter months should not be a problem if you can provide them with the minimum temperature they need. On no account should the plants be left on windowsills. If possible, put the pots on a table in the center of the room and water so that the potting soil is very moist.

The summer fishing expedition

Leaving plants during the summer months is much more of a problem because the plants are actively growing and their water requirements are much greater than during the winter months. If your holiday is for more than a week, the most satisfactory solution is to ask your neighbor to drop in occasionally and look after them. If your neighbor has a wooden thumb for plants, make sure that the dangers of overwatering are impressed upon him or her.

Back outdoors for a good garden clean-up

It was necessary to keep on about indoor plants to make sure you'd have those glorious blooms at holiday time, but the latter part of October is garden-closing time.

While we get some downpours come fall, we also get many beautiful days, so before mid-November, let's get everything tidy, making it that much easier in spring.

I spade under all the old plants that have been touched by the first frost of fall. The alternative is to gather the old plants and leaves, making sure to discard anything infested with insects or disease, and composting this waste with a composter or white lime to make good garden manure.

I find that by turning under all the leaves and old annual plants, the manure forms quickly in the soil, meaning less work and rich soil next spring.

I leave my garden in its turned-over state over winter, and in the spring I fork in bonemeal or more chicken or mushroom manure just prior to raking it level and doing the planting.

While cleaning about the garden, it's well to discard or move to a dry place old boards or wood which may have been left lying about. These chunks of wood or board will only provide a hiding place over winter for grubs, slugs, earwigs, and other pests.

It's still too early for my annual pruning job, but I do cut off any diseased branches or twigs from the plum or cherry trees. Also, I cut back some of the leggy stems with spent blooms from the rose bushes. While I'm at it, I'll cut back some of the laurel, juniper, and hydrangeas. Only the stems that have bloomed are cut out from the hydrangea. I burn the whole lot except for the old hydrangea blooms, which usually have 1 to 15 inch (2.5 to 38 centimeter) stems. These are bunched and hung to dry from the rafters in my airy garage. The hydrangea blooms will make lovely winter bouquets in varying shades of blue, lavender, and plum.

It's time to dig up all the gladiolus and dahlia tubers. The gladioluses are washed with the hose, though I do not remove the tops until probably a month from now, at which time they'll twist off clean and easy.

I store the gladiolus corms in a dry, warm place in the basement. I've made a few wire-bottomed boxes which are set on a couple of small blocks of wood to allow plenty of air circulation through them. They're also dusted lightly with a bulb dust to prevent bugs and disease.

The dahlias are left to dry quickly, but while the tops are cut off shortly after digging, I do not shake off all the dirt but instead dust the cluster of tubers, after they've dried, with a bulb dust and place them in boxes covered with dry peat moss. The boxes are kept in my crawlspace where it's cooler.

My lawn is fairly young, so I give it a final cutting, not too low, and cover it with a generous application, 50 pounds (23 kilograms) for every 1500 square feet (135 square meters) of white agricultural lime. In about 2 weeks, I'll also apply 40 pounds (18 kilograms) to every 2500 square feet (225 square meters) of fall-spring fertilizer, 2-14-6, which also has 200 pounds (91 kilograms) of sulphur and 40 pounds (18 kilograms) of magnesium to every ton. This fertilizer has just enough nitrogen to keep the lawn winter green, plus plenty of phosphate to allow for strong, winter root growth, as well as potash to make it tough and hardy. As important, this fertilizer has plenty of sulphur to help prevent winter diseases. This is especially important should we get much snow. Lots of magnesium makes it still greener and hardy against frost and cold winter.

For older lawns, the preparation is somewhat more complicated. Rent an aerator which punches plenty of holes through the matted roots and throws out the plugs. Then apply the fall-spring fertilizer and follow it with a light, but complete, dressing of a mixture of half washed river sand and half peat moss. You should apply about 1 yard (0.9 meters) of this mix to every 2500 square feet (225 square meters) of lawn and rake it in. You should also apply the lime at the same rate I do, a week before you aerate.

I bring in a few big sacks of peat moss (you could use sawdust) and cover the crowns of all my rose bushes to a depth of 4 to 6 inches (10 to 15 centimeters). This again provides winter protection. Any tender bulbs or roots of plants left in the garden over winter get a similar dressing.

I'll also put four sturdy sticks by a palm tree and fatsia bush, so that if the real cold weather hits, I can quickly put a drop sheet, preferably burlap, or an old thin canvas or rug (if necessary plastic) right over the sticks and tie it down with twine to prevent it from blowing away. Remember, plants are better protected from freezing when there's air (preferably circulating) between the plant and the cover.

Getting flowerbeds readied for planting

The first week of October is the time to prepare flowerbeds so that you can have a patch of color from now until next year's annuals again make their glorious showing.

My fibrous begonias usually look surprisingly beautiful despite any inclement weather, but many other annuals, such as my calendula bed, the ageratum, petunias, and taller cut flowers, have seen better days and are ready for the compost pile. I'll start digging up a good part of the garden this weekend, and getting the first of the fall bulbs planted, even though the bulb planting task will stretch from now until December.

To avoid disappointment, I plan the garden planting layout now, stock up on the bulbs I will need as well as the winter-blooming pansies and wallflowers, and undertake the initial planting at the first opportunity.

Our garden around the back patio offers the greatest challenge. This is the one area which is in view every day of the year and, therefore, gives the most pleasure to us all. There I'll have a splash of winter pansies which, in a normal year, will give color from the first day they are planted right through to spring. A patch of wallflowers in both the dwarf orange siberian variety and a mix of colors in the taller type, will not only grow during the winter months, but will also provide a nice evergreen showing that produces an abundance of very fragrant bloom in April and May. At the very front, we'll have both snowdrops, chionodoxa, and winter-blooming crocus. Last year my winter-blooming crocus in the very protected spots produced their first blooms about Christmas, and they continued to bloom for weeks on end. Naturally, I'll plant a good selection of my favorite rock garden tulips and daffodils, which come in many bright colors and shapes, and begin their first showing of color in February, stretching clear through until the end of April. For that final touch of elegance, I'll have several groupings of tall Darwin hybrid tulips, parrot and lily-flowered tulips, and, of course, the very reliable, fragrant narcissuses and daffodils.

In the middle of my front patio is a large, raised planter from which the geraniums will be removed now. Their places will be taken by hyacinths. The hyacinths provide so much fragrance that the front patio probably gets more attention in spring than at any other time of the year.

We have a large flowerbed in the center of the lawn, which, in spring, is of special interest to the connoisseur, as it will display large groupings of dwarf, double early, and tall double late tulips, as well as such specialty items as fancy parrot tulips and novelty green tulips.

The side flowerbeds will be reserved for a smashing array of grape hyacinths in front, with red emperor tulips immediately behind, and tall King Alfred golden daffodils at the very back. These all come into bloom at the same time, giving a spectacular showing of color for the entire month of March (an otherwise dreary month).

The key to success is planting at the first opportunity, and using some bulb dust and bulb food to give a lasting supply of nutrients and protection. Don't forget to stock up early to avoid the disappointment of finding that the choicest varieties are sold out.

Soil pits for storing surplus

Gardeners everywhere are now collecting the last of the harvest from the vegetable garden. The potatoes can be stored in a root cellar (if you are lucky enough to have one), or they can be kept in a dark, cool basement, provided the area is frost-free. Failing that, potatoes and other root crops such as beets, carrots, turnips, parsnips, rutabagas, etc., can be stored in soil pits. The soil pits are prepared by digging a foot into the ground in a well drained area, placing the rootcrops in the pit, and mounding the sides about a good foot above ground level. Stick a plastic vent pipe or two into the middle of the pile, and about 2 feet (60 centimeters) above the pile. Cover the mound, preferably with dry straw, to a depth of 6 inches (15 centimeters). I've used newspapers to a depth of 2 inches (5 centimeters) when straw wasn't available. Then cover the straw with about a 6 inch (15 centimeter) layer of dirt. You can dig out of the pit all winter long and into spring, replacing the covering whenever sufficient potatoes or carrots have been removed. It is important to store only sound, healthy roots or tubers and make sure they do not become damp. Damaged roots and tubers are the first to contract such destructive diseases as soft rot, gangrene, or sclerotinia rot. Again, store only sound, healthy roots and tubers, and make sure the storage area is airy and frost-free.

The last tomatoes on the vine will not ripen outside at this time of year. Therefore, the whole vines can be pulled from the ground and hung from a ceiling in the basement or garage, frost-free, to ripen indoors. Fruit affected by disease often will not show the symptoms until brought indoors. The most common nuisance is potatoe blight, which is evident by the forming of a brown, shrunken area on the fruit. The affected tomato is soon completely rotten. The only remedy is to destroy the diseased fruit.

Starting cleanup

You'll soon be raking leaves. Remember to burn the leaves from under the fruit trees to deter the spread and threat of apple scab and other fungus problems that troubled your fruit this year. Rake leaves from under the rose bushes and burn these as well. The maple leaves, alder, and birch may be placed in the compost box to ensure a plentiful supply of good compost manure for next year.

Whether your compost heap is a useful source of humus-making manure or an evil-smelling rubbish dump at the end of the garden depends upon following one simple rule. Look after the bacteria and they will look after your compost. Waste plant material is converted into compost by bacteria, and their simple needs are air, moisture, nitrogen, and lime. To make sure there is enough air present, mix all of the vegetable matter together before putting it on the heap. Grass clippings should be mixed with more bulky materials so that the layer doesn't become too compressed. Make sure the air is not driven out by making the heap too big, 3 feet wide and 3 feet high (15 centimeters by15 centimeters) is quite enough!

To provide the bacteria with enough moisture, all materials put into the heap should be wet, but not soggy. The need of the bacteria for nitrogen and lime has to be met by sprinkling the appropriate dressing over the surface. You can use Rot-It, Fertosan, or some similar composting medium. White lime is also extensively used.

Cheer up winter days by bringing spring indoors

I am happy to see more and more gardeners try their hand at growing bulbs indoors. It is really quite easy once you get the hang of it. In Europe, you can hardly find a window in winter without a pot of blooming crocus, hyacinths, daffodils, or tulips and every house has a lovely amaryllis at Christmas. There's something very special about flowerbulbs indoors; it brings spring over and over to otherwise dreary winter months.

In the previous chapter, I presented some of the basic rules and now I want to elaborate specifically on some of the less known, though possibly more enjoyable approaches to having spring all winter.

Crocus   Fill a shallow bowl or dish (best about 2 inches [5 centimeters] in depth) with washed gravel or rocks. Fill with water until it reaches the top of the gravel. Set your crocus bulbs on top of the gravel, pushing them in about one quarter inch (0.6 centimeters). Plant the bulbs close together—about a half inch (1.3 centimeters) in between each—to create a mass of bloom and offer each other support.

Now, set the bowl in a dark and cool cupboard or some cool spot in the garage or basement—cool but frost free. Add only sufficient water now and again to keep the water level in the bowl to just below the bulbs.

In about 14 days the bulbs will begin to shoot roots and these will grow quickly to create a mass of roots in the bowl. The root growth is especially effective if you use a glass see-through bowl. The shoots (spikes) will soon begin to appear. But don't let this fool you into bringing them indoors or into your living room right away. You must wait until the shoots are about 3 to 4 inches (7 to 10 centimeters) high and the flowerheads are clearly visible inside the shoot. Again, do not forget to continually add water because if they once dry out, they simply cannot produce flowers.

Crocus bulbs (corms) can also be grown on soil, but

in that case, you would plant in the pot (with drainage) so that the bulbs are just slightly below the surface of the soil. Bury the pot outside in the garden so that the pot is covered with 4 to 5 inches (10 to 13 centimeters) of soil, or set on top of the ground and cover with a generous mound of peat moss or sawdust. Leave the pots until January and then bring indoors.

Hyacinth　You may follow the same procedure as outlined above for hyacinths, except that the hyacinths would be spaced about 1½ inches (4 centimeters) apart in the bowl or pot. The bowl or pot should have a depth of preferably 4 inches (10 centimeters). The bulbs are then set into the gravel 1 inch (2.5 centimeters), or, if using soil, to a depth just below the tip of the bulb.

Hyacinths purchased for this purpose must be the forcing size and type and not those purchased for regular garden planting.

There are those hyacinth bulbs especially treated for Christmas flowering, and they are brought into the living room about December 1. There are also those for Valentine blooming which are brought in about mid-January.

Hyacinths can also be grown in water by using special hyacinth vases (with narrow necks) which support the bulb to a fraction of an inch above the water level; jam jars or wine glasses may do. Remember, the roots will reach for the water if the water is close enough, and, once in the water, the roots will continue to grow without rotting. The best distance between bulb and water is 1 millimeter or about the thickness of a dime.

Remember to keep adding the water carefully so as to maintain a proper level.

Narcissus　Another most rewarding crop of very fragrant blooms which can be grown exactly as the crocus and hyacinth are the narcissis varieties called paperwhite, grand soleil d'or, and cragford. Find yourself a shallow bowl, approximately 4 inches deep and 8 inches across (10 centimeters by 20 centimeters), and preferably glass so that you can watch the root growth. Fill the bowl with pebbles (white pebbles are most attractive) to 1 inch (2.5 centimeters) below the rim of the bowl. Set five bulbs, evenly spaced in the bowl and to a depth of half the bulb. Fill the bowl with water to a level just below the bottom of the bulb and set the bowl in a dark closet, basement, or garage, frost-free with a temperature of preferably 40-50° F (5-10° C). If you do not have a dark place, try a black plastic bag covering the bowl. Check the water-level once a week and add more as needed to keep the level up. Leave in the dark for about 6 weeks and then bring it out, placing the bowl first in a partly shaded area in the house and then in the full light.

There are many other varieties of daffodils and narcissuses that can be grown indoors, but these are better grown on soil and dug in or under, as described for crocus bulbs, and brought into the house any time.

Tulip   Last, but not least, are tulips. Tulips are grown in soil (not gravel) in pots. The pots should be about 4 inches (10 centimeters) deep and have proper drainage holes. The bulbs are planted halfway into the soil and about 1 inch (2.5 centimeters) apart. The pots are buried in the garden so that there is about a 6-inch (15-centimeter) soil cover, or they are placed in a sheltered spot, and covered with a mound of peat moss or sawdust.

Sometimes, for those lucky people with a root cellar or cool, dark, frost-free basement or crawlspace, burying is not required as they can be simply set there and watered occasionally to prevent drying out. The Christmas flowering varieties such as the kaufmanniana or certain varieties of fosteriana, can be brought indoors December 1, while the flowering varieties such as double or single early tulips can be brought in starting the 14th, depending on when you want the blooms, as it usually takes a month indoors before they appear.

The later tulips and daffodils are brought indoors from late January on.

October planting for Christmas blooms

The kaufmanniana tulips can be grown in potting soil in a shallow pot or, as is so often done in Europe, in a planter sleigh-shaped to add to the Christmas spirit.

Try a small pot of crocus, glory of the snow, or Siberian squills to provide another touch of spring on the Christmas table. These little bulbs only need to be in the dark for a total of about 4 weeks.

Homebaked cookies and homemade jams are always appreciated as Christmas gifts. For those who like to give something special, why not try some spring flowers in a special planter?

Bulbs can be forced more easily for January and February since there is more time and the selection is considerably expanded by many more varieties of early tulips, fragrant narcissuses, and golden daffodils. For these later varieties, the period of darkness is usually from 10 to 12 weeks.

Perennials must be planted now

Fall is not just a time for planting the spring flowering bulbs; it is also a time to plant the spring flowering perennials.

The most popular of the spring bulb companion flowering plants are the wallflowers (*cheiranthus*).

The wallflower is an evergreen plant which is hardy for our area and somewhat woody. Wallflowers were first discovered on the Canary Islands and in the Mediterranean area. Later, they were brought to England where the hybridist did a marvelous job producing numerous varieties in many colors from primrose to dark red, yellow, orange, and purple.

The regular wallflowers grow to an average height of about 18 inches (45 centimeters), and, though attractively green throughout winter, are really a long lasting show of lovely fragrant blooms from April until June, with the Siberian wallflower blooming as early as March.

Wallflowers can be started from seed in June or July outdoors. In a finely prepared ground, sow them about a quarter-inch (0.6 centimeters) deep. When the seedlings are 2 to 3 inches (5 to 7 centimeters) high, they are transplanted to about 9 inches (23 centimeters) apart and left until October, at which time they're planted in their permanent spots. The plants can stand considerable frost but during a long cold snap some fir branches or cedar boughs laid lightly over the plants will provide the necessary protection.

The Siberian wallflower bears a profusion of orange or yellow flowers in March through May that are colorful and fragrant.

They're excellent to plant as a border or between your Darwin tulips. Also, the Siberian wallflower is much hardier than the English types and grows to only about 12 inches (30 centimeters) high.

Another type of increasingly popular wallflower is the alpine (or *Cheiranthus alpinus*). They are best suited for rock gardens.

All wallflowers are available at nurseries or garden centers in the fall. They can be planted during October and November. Wallflowers are actually perennial, but most people treat then as biennials.

One of my favorite plants, which has established itself naturally throughout my garden, is the forget-me-not (*Myosotis*). They reseed themselves quickly and there are waves of blue blooms everywhere, especially in those areas where other plantings are difficult.

The seed is sown in June or July about 1 inch (2.5 centimeters) deep in well-worked soil. As soon as the seedlings are of sufficient size, they should be thinned or transplanted to about 6 inches (15 centimeters) apart. In the fall they are moved to their permanent spots.

The forget-me-nots are delightful flowering plants, ideal for naturalizing in informal areas or the garden—in the shrubbery, by the sidewalk, or in open spaces among trees.

My forget-me-nots thrive well in sun or partial shade, and even the small plants, put out in October and November, make for large bushy clusters of dainty bloom in spring. The forget-me-nots bloom long, from March until June. They're available at stores throughout October.

At the Parliament Buildings, they've just finished planting primroses amongst the low bushes and in the planters. They'll produce a rainbow of colors beginning in very early spring and going right through until summer.

The primroses and polyanthuses in the beds at the buildings are in the sun, but they'll do equally well or generally much better when planted in semi-shade. Plant under the trees and bushes or in planters and pots.

You can start your own primroses from seed in June-July or you can buy the plants ready-grown from your garden center in the fall.

One of the most popular plantings for all winter, spring, and summer bloom are the alpine ice pansies. These pansies are somewhat smaller in bloom than the regular types. They are a clear color—that is, they have no face—and come in shades of blue, yellow, or white. Planted now in rockery, planter, border, or amongst your bulbs, they'll be at their very best come early spring.

October is also heather planting time. Heather is available in many varieties of colors, and you can purchase spring, summer, fall, or winter flowering varieties.

My favorite is the winter blooming Mediterranean heather which is just now showing a bit of color in my garden. My winter blooming Mediterranean heathers are up to 3 feet (90 centimeters) across and will bloom from now until next April regardless of weather, even in the snow. If you plant now, they will root well over the winter and grow into big bushes a year from now.

Every year millions of houseplants die needlessly

You don't need to read books to learn about the beauty, variety, and popularity of house plants; just look around you. Everywhere you will find them, the popular indoor gardens in public buildings, the many pots on windowsills, and scores of colorful varieties offered for sale in garden shops.

Most everyone loves houseplants, yet millions of them die needlessly every year. You have to face the fact that your house is not a particularly good home for the philodendron, otherwise resident in the trees of moist but warm Central America, or the rubber trees from Brazil. Actually, most plants would prefer the moist, bright air of a well-lit laundry. You can't just leave them to look after themselves; each plant needs care and each variety has its own particular requirements.

Basic rules for houseplants

Don't drown houseplants; roots need air as well as water. Keeping the potting soil soaked at all times means certain death for most plants. You must learn how to water properly.

Without water a houseplant will die. This may take place in a single day, in the case of a seedling in sandy soil, or it may take months if the plant has fleshy leaves.

Many indoor gardeners lovingly give daily dribbles of water. They fail to cut down on the frequency of watering once winter arrives and they immediatley assume that the plant is thirsty, whenever leaves wilt or turn yellow. This produces a sour, soggy soil in which practically no houseplant can survive. Waterlogging kills by preventing oxygen from getting to the roots and by encouraging root rotting diseases. More plants die through overwatering than any other cause; they are killed by kindness.

Plants differ from one to another as to their basic water requirements. The proper frequency of watering varies according to circumstances such as the size of the plant, the size of the pot, the environment, and especially the time of year. Your best guide is to watch the plant closely and test with your finger.

The dry in winter plants are the cactuses and succulents. During the active growing season, from spring to fall, these plants should be treated as the moist-dry plants, but in winter the soil should be allowed to dry almost completely.

The moist-dry plants include most foliage plants. The standard recommendation is to water thoroughly and often between spring and fall and to water sparingly in winter, letting the top 1 or 2 inches (2.5 to 5 centimeters) in large pots dry out each time between waterings.

The moist at all times group includes most flowering plants. The soil is kept moist, but not wet, at all times. The recommendation here is to water each time the surface becomes dry, but never frequently enough to keep the soil permanently wet.

Very few plants belong in the wet at all times group. Water thoroughly and frequently enough to keep the soil wet, not just moist. Examples: azaleas and cypprus, cyclamen, and cinneraria.

Danger signs of wrong watering

Too little Leaves wilt, become limp; little or no growth; flowers fall or fade quickly; lower leaves curl, yellow; leaf edges turn brown and dry; oldest leaves fall.

Too much Leaves become limp, soft; rotten areas; little or no growth; flowers moldy; leaves curl, yellow, wilt; leaf-tips turn brown; old and young leaves fall.

Our tap water is suitable for all plants. It is best for the water to stand overnight to reach room temperature. This standing period is especially important for delicate varieties. I never give my plants cold tap water. I don't have a problem with chlorine as I have an excellent well, but I use only tepid water. The old-time gardener used rainwater, and I still recommend this highly, but be sure is isn't stagnant.

USE SEPARATE POCKETS TO GROUP HERBS AND OTHER PLANTS

It's difficult to tell when to water, since obviously this depends on the plant, the environment, and the time of year. For most plants, I still prefer my number one moisture meter, my forefinger. Obviously, some plants need more water than others, and it is actually hard to overwater during the peak of the growing season in summer, but still my forefinger is the most reliable. I stick it in the pot—that is, the larger pots—to a depth of 2 inches (5 centimeters), and if it's dry, then it needs a good watering. The most important exceptions are the cactuses and succulents in winter. If the room is cool, leave them alone, unless there are signs of shriveling.

As I've said, roots need air as well as water, which means that the soil should be moist, but not saturated. Some plants need a partial drying-out period between waterings; others do not. All will need less water during the resting period.

You must never allow watering to become a regular routine whereby the pots are filled up every Sunday. The correct water break will vary greatly, depending on variety, time of year, and where the plant sits.

Thick or fleshy-leaved plants can tolerate much drier conditions than thin-leaved plants, and a rooted cutting will take up much less water than a mature plant. With any plant, the layers, the leaf surface, and the rate of growth will determine the need for watering. In winter, growth slows and may stop; overwatering must be avoided during this resting season. Until new growth starts in the spring, watering 2 to 3 times a month is usually sufficient. During the spring and summer, watering will be necessary 2 to 3 times a week.

As the temperature and the light intensity increases, so does the need to water. Plants in small pots and those which are pot bound need more frequent watering than those in large containers or ones which have been recently potted. Plants in clay pots need water more often than those in plastic pots.

When watering, use a can with a long spout. Insert the end of the spout under the leaves and pour the water steadily and gently. Water until the soil is thoroughly moistened; you can stop when it comes out the bottom. Never water on foliage in full sun as splashed leaves may be scorched. In winter, water in the morning if the room is unheated. This will prevent shock to the roots.

If a plant is very dry and the water runs straight through, try watering by immersion in a bucket or bath of water. Plants such as African violets, gloxinias, and cyclamen, which do not like water on their leaves or crowns, can be watered from below by immersion of the pots in water to just below the level of the soil and leaving them to soak until the surface glistens. Allow them to drain and then return the pots to their growing spots.

Your plants don't need tropical temperatures

The natural home of most indoor plants is the tropics. And, for the most part, in our region they are raised commercially in greenhouses. These two facts have given rise to the widespread belief that high temperatures are essential in the proper growing of houseplants.

Very few types will grow satisfactorily at temperatures above 75° F (25°C) in room conditions. Because the amount of light falling on the leaves and the amount of moisture in the air are far less in a room than outdoors in the tropics or in the greenhouse, the need for heat is correspondingly less.

Most indoor plants do well if the temperature is kept within the 55-75° F (12-25° C) range. Most types will grow quite happily in rooms which are a little too cool for human comfort. There are exceptions to this general rule; many flowering plants and some foliage houseplants need much cooler conditions with a maximum temperature of 60° F (15° C) in winter. At the other end of the scale, the tender varieties require a minimum of 60° F (15° C). With warmth- and moisture-loving plants, the pots can be placed in a pebble tray in a warm spot. A pebble tray is a shallow, 2-inch (5-centimeter) tray with a 1-inch (2.5-centimeter) layer of pebbles on the bottom that is kept wet at all times. The water level must not cover the top of the gravel. Watering is simple; allow excess water to run out of the pots and into the gravel. If you have had difficulty growing African violets, try this pebble method—you'll be amazed.

Most plants are remarkably tough and will survive temperatures slightly above or below the preferred range for short periods. The real enemy is temperature changes. Plants do appreciate a drop of 5-10° F (2-5° C) at night but a sudden cooling down can be damaging or fatal. Cactuses do not have this same problem. They are desert plants accustomed to day and night temperature changes.

Danger signs of wrong temperatures

Too warm   Flowers short-lived; spindly growth in good light, winter or spring; lower leaves wilt; leaf edges turn brown; bottom leaves fall.

Too cold   Leaf curl followed by browning and leaf fall.

Sudden temperature change   Rapid yellowing followed by leaf fall.

Moist air a must for houseplant success

Cold air requires only a small amount of humidity before it becomes saturated; that's why on an average winter day the air is moist. When you turn on a hot air furnace to warm up this cold air, its capacity to hold water vapor is greatly increased. As the room becomes comfortable, the amount of humidity in the air is no longer enough to keep it moist. The air becomes dry; the relative humidity falls.

The hot air furnace in the middle of winter can produce air with a relative humidity of the Sahara Desert. Few plants actually like such conditions; many foliage plants and most flowering plants will suffer if you don't do something to increase the humidity around the plant. You can of course, avoid the problem by finding a moist place for your plants, such as the kitchen or the bathroom, but the other rooms will have a dry atmosphere. You can use a humidifier to increase the humidity in the whole room, but it is more usual to use one or more of the methods below to produce a moist microclimate around the plant while the atmosphere in the rest of the room remains dry.

Misting   Use a mister to spray the leaves. It is best to use tepid water, and under cool temperatures, do this job in the morning so that the foliage will be dry before evening. Cover the whole plant. Do not mist when the foliage is exposed to bright sunlight. Misting does more than provide a temporary increase in humidity; it also has a cooling effect on hot, sunny days, discourages red spider mite, and removes the dust from the leaves.

Grouping   Plants grown in pot groups and indoor planters have the benefit of increased moisture arising from damp soil and the foliage of surrounding plants. The air trapped between them wil have a higher relative humidity than the atmosphere around an isolated plant.

Double potting   Use an outer waterproof jardeniere and fill the space between the pot and the jardeniere with moist peat. Keep this packing material thoroughly and continually moist so that there will always be a surface layer of moisture to evaporate and raise the relative humidity. Double potting does more than just raise the humidity. It also provides a moisture reservoir below the pot and insulates the soil inside the pot from sudden changes in temperature.

Relative humidity and what it means to your plants

Leaf tips will shrivel and turn brown if there is too little humidity. Buds and flowers will fall, leaf edges will turn yellow,

MAINTAINING HUMIDITY

DAILY MISTING

PEBBLE TRAY

and wilting will occur. If the plant is very sensitive to dry air, leaves will fall.

Houseplants need less warm air and more moist air than expected. Thin leaves need more humidity in the air than thick leaves. If your room has hot air vents, be sure to follow one or several of the methods suggested previously for raising the relative humidity.

Humidity percentages

    100% - Saturated air.

70 - 90% - Jungle air. Summer greenhouse in our area.

40 - 60% - Summer day in our region and also the best range for indoor plants in room conditions.

10 - 30% - Desert air. Winter, centrally heated conditions in our region.

      0% - Bone-dry air, not found in nature.

Proper use of fertilizer needed for healthy plants

All plants everywhere need an adequate supply of nitrogen, phosphates, and potash, as well as small amounts of trace elements. Given this you will be rewarded with healthy growth and full-sized flowers and leaves.

Outside, it is usual to apply fertilizers to add to the soil's natural resources, but even if these are absent the plants can continue to draw on the soil's supply of nutrients by sending out new roots. Indoors the situation is quite different. The soil in the pot contains a very limited amount of food, and this is continually depleted by the roots of the plant and by leaching through the drainage holes. Once the nutrient supply is gone you must feed regularly when the plant is growing. Cactuses can survive for a long time without any feeding, but strong foliage plants coming into bloom are seriously affected if not fed.

Too little fertilizer Slow growth, little resistance to pests and diseases. Leaves pale, washed out appearance, yellow spotting may be present. Flowers absent or small and poorly colored. Stems weak; early dropping of lower leaves.

Too much fertilizer Leaves wilted. White crust on surface of the potting soil. Growth lanky and weak. Crisp brown spots, scorched edges.

Q: **How do I get rid of mealybugs on my indoor plants?**
A: Try Safer's Insecticidal soap. It works well in our greenhouses.

Q: **I would like you to recomend some shrubs for containers on my balconies to give me privacy.**
A: The thuja smarag grows compact and narrow to about 5 or 6 feet (1.5 to 2 meters) and is perfectly hardy. I think you'll like it.

Q: **I have an aglaonema plant, but it's not doing well. It's not in bright light, which I was told to avoid. What's wrong?**
A: True, the aglaonema thrives in poorly lit locations but more than just lighting affects this plant. It should be grown in a shallow pot. It needs moist air and the leaves misted regularly. Surrounding the pot with damp peat moss is a good idea for its welfare. Air must not be too dry or too cool, and it must not be subjected to drafts. Check also at the base of the leaf stocks for mealybug. Should the light be a little bright, you could also have red spider mites.

November

Trees and bushes splash a blaze of color in fall

It is true that the central and eastern regions of North America have the wildest display of fall colors, but the northwest is spectacular too.

There is nothing more beautiful than splashes of yellow, orange, and red surrounded by lush evergreens. We have a milder climate in which to enjoy the scenery too.

Everywhere in the garden or in the wilds the colors provide settings of beauty and tranquility that brighten the shortening days. The best among plants with bright foliage in the fall are the acid-soil lovers. These include azaleas, blueberries, sour-wood, and deciduous lily of the valley bush. Unlike the broad-leaved acid-loving trees and shrubs, they like the sun and are hardy and pest-free.

There are a number of hardwood trees with beautiful fall colors. The most colorful and most popular of hardwoods is the vine maple. The sugar maple, though not as well known here, is also a brilliant and beautiful tree.

We must not overlook the beautiful scarlet oaks and the much smaller sumac trees. Both add a bright spot to any fall garden and their foliage is long-lasting.

One of my most favorite and one of the most rewarding small trees is the liquidamber or the sweet gum tree. There are several varieties of these: some have leaves of one color, while others have a mixture of colors. The sweet gum also has a corky bark, which in itself makes the tree unusual.

A group of trees common to our area are the dogwoods. Our native dogwood produces the most superior blooms by far, and they're produced in great abundance in the spring and again in the fall.

The most colorful dogwood for foliage is the florida (many flowers) dogwood. The white flowering florida dogwood has brilliant red foliage, while the pink and red flowering dogwoods have a lovely purple foliage in fall.

In my garden, the flowering crab and mountain ash trees give a double value during the fall and winter months. Not only do they provide shades of gold when the leaves begin to color, but after the leaves have dropped I have the bright orange crabapple and the red ash berries, both of which stay on until the birds begin to feast on them in the early winter.

Because of the color of both the foliage and the bark in the fall, the shrub dogwoods are growing in popularity. The silver and gold variegated-leaved varieties have a maroon-red bark, the green-leaved osier dogwood has brilliant red bark, and Flaviramea has a golden bark.

These shrubs make an oustanding show in the winter garden. Another showpiece is witch hazel. It has bright yellow leaves during the fall that drop off early in November and then expose thick, furry, attractive flower buds, which, regardless of weather, unfurl come January and provide a fascinating display of fragrant, midwinter, yellow, spidery-looking blooms.

Along with my witch hazel, I really enjoy the very fragrant *Viburnum fragrans,* which produces an almost snowball-like, white-fringed pink bloom in later winter and early spring, as well as the evergreen *Viburnum tinus,* which has lovely reddish flowerbuds all winter, which, when they open in February, expose flat blooms, changing from pink to white.

In front of my holly tree, which is loaded with red Christmas berries, stand my Christmas roses, the Oregon grape with its purple berries, and several varieties of low-spreading cotoneasters with berries from deep red to a pleasant orange. But most showy is the pyracantha.

My pyracantha, commonly known as firethorn, is not the red but the orange-berried variety, and it's so loaded that you really can't even detect the evergreen foliage. Barberry plants are also strikingly lovely, but the dwarf Japanese maple takes no back seat.

There are numerous bright-colored vines. The Boston and the

Virginia creeper are tremendously colorful in foliage, but the climbing hydrangea holds its own by displaying rich brown peeling bark on twisted stems.

We all enjoy the bright silver bark of birch trees, which come in both the upright and weeping varieties; the shiny gold of the weeping willows; and the unusual bark of the peeling mahogany cherry. But there are few things more lovely than the first show of the pussy willows, the breaking of the extremely fragrant February daphne, and the sure sign of spring, early forsythia.

There's much more that can be said about the beauties of a fall and winter garden, but just remember that every season has its beauty and our seasons and expanses of wilderness areas provide the greatest beauty anywhere in the world.

The mountain ash is a popular fall tree with its colorful foliage and bright berries.

Some more on pruning

I have previously written about pruning, but since it's one of the most important things in a good garden, I would like to review some of the basics once again.

By now, you know the purposes of pruning are varied: to keep plants healthy, to restrict or to promote growth, to encourage blooming, or to repair damage.

Sometimes pruning is needed to bring back old or overgrown trees or shrubs and sometimes to encourage young plants to take on a certain form. The orchardist prunes to get bigger and better fruit and to prolong the life of his trees, while the rose grower prunes for bigger and better blooms. Hedges are pruned to make them thick and effective, but in every case the purpose of the pruning is to get more out of the plant.

Pruning is really an everyday thing. Whenever you pinch back a snapdragon or petunia, it branches to produce more blooms. Whenever you cut a vase of forsythia blooms from your favorite bush, it allows more sideshoots to develop. This will give more branches to cut next year. Every gardener is pruning even if only removing the dead blooms.

There is pruning to be done in every season. The beauty of a Japanese garden lies in its excellent maintenance. Pruning is continuous, carried on with thumbnail and fingernail. Every new shoot is nipped at just the proper time to give plants the groomed look too seldom seen in our own gardens.

Maybe the term "green thumb" came from the color of the pinching fingers of a good gardener. This thumb is truly green, stained from the plant juice picked up as he bends down to pinch a shoot or remove some dead blooms.

A lovely, lush spreading juniper planted near the sidewalk at the front of your house can get so big in a few years that it would have to be removed or cut back so severely that its plumey grace would be lost. A little yearly maintenance pruning can keep it in hand and preserve its natural beauty.

A lilac bush from the nursery with three or four sturdy canes and a few smaller shoots apparently thrives untouched in the shrub garden. Then in about five years it draws attention because it looks straggly, flowers are smaller, the trunk is insect-riddled, and a lot of suckers have shot up all around, keeping out light and air. Regular pruning could have kept the trunk clear of suckers and the tops low enough to be seen.

You planted a privet hedge and failed to prune it back for three or four years but now are faced with a broad, dense top and a bunch of bare stalks lower down. The effect is unsightly and the condition unhealthy. Yearly pruning would have produced thick growth, and, if the top had been kept narrower than the base, the foliage would not have been deprived of light.

If you have trees that have already been left for a number of years and are now a mass of spindly suckers and wrist-thick center trunks, where do you start?

First, remove all old and diseased wood. Second, cut back promising, healthy wood to encourage branching. Finally, thin the sucker growth, leaving a few shoots to keep young growth coming on. The multitrunks will require a saw, and to make room for the saw you may have to remove some branches that you would prefer to keep. Any cut branch over 1 inch (2.5 centimeters) should be painted with a tree paint or tree emulsion to prevent dry rot or bleeding.

The time to prune the trees or to hand-prune the shrubs is winter, or from now on.

Handle with care the younger shoots or those with smooth, usually light, bark.

Some specific targets for your pruning tools

If your privet or laurel hedge has gone all straggly, as many of them do, cut it to the ground or at least to very short stubs, about 8 inches (20 centimeters), and do so in about late February. Again, I paint with a tree emulsion all cuts over 1 inch (2.5 centimeters) in diameter, as this prevents bleeding and die-back.

Immediately after the pruning, give the whole hedge a good feeding with a regular 13-5-7 "treat" fertilizer and water well.

New shoots will soon break from the old crowns, and, if these are then kept sheared throughout the summer, your hedge will rebuild itself quickly. Remember in future to do regular pruning to prevent this straggliness.

Rhododendrons and azaleas, especially the former, often take on a straggly look. Again, cut these back as you would a hedge, though if the plant is covered with buds you may want to wait until after blooming. Paint all the cuts with tree emulsion and, again, feed and water well, using a specially formulated acid fertilizer.

My heather is trimmed back after it finishes blooming, and, as most of it is winter flowering, this means waiting until April. Once again, follow with a good feeding.

I really have to keep my wisteria vine pruned back or it would walk away with the clothesline pole. I maintain the main trunk stems and avoid too many laterals. During the summer I prune back continuously all the reaching tendrils before they get woody and entwined.

There is really no effective way to trim your spruce or other lawn trees. The only way to ensure the health and good looks of a fine blue spruce or specimen pine is to attend to maintenance pruning; to regularly pinch the new growth especially; to spray regularly in spring, summer, and fall against red spider or aphids, and to feed every spring.

Multiple-trunk evergreens such as junipers, cedars and cypresses can and should be trimmed. Regular early fall trimming is my most successful approach, though junipers could also be trimmed in early spring. If these evergreens get out of hand and become straggly, you can cut them back quite severely, but never cut beyond green foliage. As long as there is a wisp of green, it will grow to replace a branch that has been removed.

Fruit-bearing plants need constant rejuvenation. A good pattern of maintenance pruning usually results in continuous replacement of old wood with younger, more productive wood. With cane fruits, most canes should be removed as soon as they have borne fruit. Grape vines are cut back every year to just a few ends on year-old canes. This provides a good crop.

There are many free pamphlets available at your local garden shop, and there are also excellent books to purchase at reasonable prices, all good insurance to provide you a greater return from fruit trees or bushes and a more attractive garden of trees and bushes, with an abundance of bloom for your pleasure.

Also consider what it does to the value of your real estate. All real estate sales people will tell you that treed lots and good landscaping impress potential buyers.

Dried flowers and branches make great indoor decoration

Looking around my garden in late fall, I usually see many still-good-looking large blue, purple and lavender blooms on my hydrangea bushes.

I cut them with good long stems. Because the stems with blooms will not bloom the following year, they should be pruned anyway. Then I place the hydrangeas in a vase without water and have a lovely giant bouquet all winter, as hydrangeas dry very quickly.

The choice of flowers and branches that can be dried to bring pleasure all winter is enormous.

Consider cones, unusual branches of shrubs and trees, dried stalks, pieces of bark, and driftwood. You can make all sorts of lovely arrangements to suit every spot in your home.

A few of the more popular varieties are baby's breath, candytuft seed pods, cupid's dart seedpods, Chinese lanterns, dusty miller, echinops (blueball), goldenrod, grains such as barley, wheat, oats, and wild grains or grasses, honesty (money plant), milkweed pods, poppy seedpods, onion tops, pussy willows, dried pampas grass, strawflowers, teasels, and bull-rushes (pick when they're young, even green; they'll turn brown).

Sweet corn tops make a nice addition to a large bouquet when lightly touched with gold spray. Dried cobs of the multicolored Indian corn are a traditional fall decoration.

Try drying evergreen branches, twigs, or boughs and ferns. Lay the branches, boughs, or fronds flat in a container with one-third

DRIED FALL BOUQUET

CHINESE LANTERN

PUSSYWILLOW

glycerin and two-thirds water for two or three days. They'll keep their color.

Roses too will dry; it just takes a little work. Put a mixture of one-half borax and one-half fine sand into the centers and gently cover them with the mixture. Leave until the petals feel dry. It is necessary to cut the stems very short and to insert wire through the length of the stem and up into the center of the flower: then bend over neatly. The wire can be covered with floral green tape when the flowers are dry.

There are many branches of leaves that can look beautiful when preserved in a solution of one-third glycerin and two-thirds water such as red maple, oak, barberry, gray birch, Japanese flowering crabapple, pyracantha (leaves will fall off but berries remain), forsythia, red-twigged cornus, yellow-twigged cornus, and beech.

When your dried flowers get dusty, dip them quickly up and down in lukewarm water to make them clean again.

Waste not, want not

My neighbors have loads of apples going to waste, and friends have bushels of pears being smashed on the ground. Let's gather all this useful fruit and make wine.

The best you can use are cooking apples, but if you have lots of apples of a dessert variety, mix some cooking apples with them.

Wipe the apples with a clean, dry cloth and cut out all the rotten pieces when slicing the fruit into small chunks. Weigh, and to every 12 pounds (5 kilograms), add a gallon (4 liters) of cold water. Cover the fermentation vessel, stir daily for five days, and then strain onto 3 pounds (1 kilogram) of sugar. Stir well to dissolve the sugar. Cover well and stir daily for a week before pouring into gallon jars.

For pear wine, prepare pears as for apple wine but do not leave the chunks exposed to the air. If you do, they will turn brown. Pop the sliced fruit into the water as soon as you can. After five days of soaking, strain the liquor onto 3 pounds (1 kilogram) of sugar and add a tablespoon of lemon juice. Cover well and leave for a week. Stir daily. Then strain through muslin into gallon jars.

It saddens me to see so much garden fruit go to waste when with a little effort you can have homemade applesauce or wine. Our ancestors would be shocked to see entire home garden crops going to waste while we're at the supermarket taking the same items off the shelves.

Q: Am I imagining things? Last summer I could have sworn that my friend's wisteria vine had more fragrance than mine. Is this possible?
A: The flavor of fruit and vegetables and the fragrance of foliage and flowers can all be influenced by growing conditions. A plant in good soil with sufficient nutrients, watered well, will carry a more intense fragrance.

Q: The new growth of my African violets keeps getting smaller and the plants grow very tight, twisted and almost white in color. What causes this, and what do I do to correct?
A: Your plants appear to have cyclamen mites. They are too small to see without magnification. Immerse your infested plant, pot and all, in water heated and held at 100°F (43°C) for 15 minutes. Or you can spray Kelthane as directed on the bottle.

Q: My wife and I are having an argument over how peanuts grow. She says they grow from flowers and I say they grow underground just like potatoes. Who wins?
A: You both do; congratulations! Your wife is right in part because after the lovely little orange flowers are pollinated, the peanuts start. The stems elongate, bending down to touch the soil (and this is where you are right), where they root themselves into the ground. Here the peanuts develop in clusters below soil level. It takes the flowers first and then the growing period underground to produce this favorite nut.

December

Limited space? Go for hanging plants

Hanging plants immediately strike you with their graceful foliage and dramatic form. Plants suspended in the air take on a special perspective and are true showpieces.

To many plant lovers, especially those with small quarters, the air provides a fine home for plants, freeing valuable floor or counter space. In addition, hanging plants offer a convenient solution to decorating problems, softening harsh wall surfaces, defining living areas, and filling empty corners. Whether you begin with one or several, hanging plants will give you a delightful swinging garden overhead.

Any indoor plant with a dangling or spreading habit can be hung to advantage. Possible locations are in or around windows, filling spaces or empty walls, or in corners and around skylights. Just be sure to hang the plants out of the way of traffic—bumping into a heavy plant is good for neither your head nor the plant.

You'll face two major challenges with hanging plants: how to suspend the plant and how to water it once it's up. Whenever possible, use plastic pots for your hanging plants. They weigh much less than clay or ceramic pots and absorb no moisture, so plants in them require less water. Most plants suitable for hanging will cover the container with foliage so you don't need to worry about spoiling your decor. If your plant does need a decorative container, be sure to choose one that is waterproof.

When spotting a place to fasten the hanger hook, you'll have no problem if you're lucky enough to have exposed beams or a panelled ceiling. Many ceilings and walls are made of gyproc, which will not hold the screws securely, so you will need to locate a ceiling joist or wall stud. You can usually locate studs by one of three methods—measure 14½ inches (37 centimeters) out from a major corner; succeeding joists and studs should fall every 16 inches (41 centimeters). You can locate the nails in studs with a magnetic stud finder, or you can knock firmly on the ceiling or

234

Bill shows a few varieties of the many hundreds of hanging
plants.

wall with the heel of your fist. A solid sound means you've located a joist; a hollow sound says keep looking. If you cannot find a stud or joist, get a toggle bolt.

Windows are the favored locations for hanging plants because windows provide good light. If you want the good light provided by a sunny window but you know your plant can't tolerate it, suspend the plant to the side of the window. For convenience, hang plants far enough away from windows to allow opening and closing of windows, curtains, or drapes.

Locations away from windows may or may not provide enough light for hanging plants. Generally speaking, a location that has enough indirect light for you to read by without turning on a lamp should be sufficient for most indoor plants.

Keep an eye out for spindly growth or dropping leaves; they are signs that your plant is receiving inadequate light. In dark areas try the varieties that survive in low light.

Watering a hanging plant can be a challenge. A watered plant will drip, presenting a threat to floors, rugs, and furniture. You can prevent drips by providing a drip saucer to catch the water; some baskets come with trays, but often these are too small. You may prefer to set the basket in a jardeniere or waterproof container as a decorative sleeve. I take most of my hanging plants down to water, set them in the sink, water in the evening, and let them drain overnight before re-hanging.

Some favorite hanging plants are listed here with a light rating: (1) sunny and plenty of light; (2) indirect light; and (3) tolerates dark.

Arrowhead vine 3
Bridal veil 2
Jasmine vine 1
Lipstick plant 2
Philodendron 2
Piggyback plant 2
Wandering jew 3

Bill shows hanging basket strawberries.

You can have sweet big strawberries summer and fall in hanging baskets.

Beauty for a favored queen

It's always interesting to brush up on garden history and learn how some of your favorite beauties were discovered.

History tells us that in 1761, Charlotte Sophia, from a small country, or duchy, north of Berlin, became the bride of George III of Great Britain and Ireland. She was a lady of no special beauty or charm but made an excellent wife for the king, as both were homely house bodies. George III's mother, the Dowager Princess of Wales, lived at Kew and was very much devoted to horticulture. Her daughter-in-law, Charlotte, apparently shared this interest, for she is remembered as a patroness of botanical and horticultural projects.

John Stuart, third Earl of Bute, dedicated his very rare botanical tables to her. Sir Joseph Banks dedicated the genus *Strelitzia* to her, and William Aiton, His Majesty's principal gardener at Kew, published a description of this plant with the name *Strelitzia reginae* (the Queen's Strelitzia), commonly called the bird of paradise.

This plant was first cultivated in 1773 by Sir Joseph Banks, who was also the informal scientific adviser to the king. The plant was first discovered and collected by Francis Masson, a Scottish gardener working at Kew who was sent to South Africa by Banks in 1772 to collect plants. Masson made a trip in December 1772, and January 1773, from Capetown, South Africa, to the Sunday River. The *Strelitzia* was a roadside weed in the region.

The bird of paradise flower has a short, stout rhizome, from which arises a cluster of bananalike leaves. The blades are about a foot (0.3 meter) long, and the leaf stalks are about 2 feet (0.6 meter) long. The flowering stalks are taller than the leaves and terminate in a more or less horizontal beaked or boatlike structure, which encloses the axis of the inflorescence proper. From this structure the individual orange and purple flowers emerge in succession.

Strange, isn't it, that a one-time weed is now a favorite and the subject for so many photographers attracted to its imposing stature?

Poinsettias, too, have a colorful history

Generations of North Americans have enjoyed poinsettia plants as one of their favorites at Christmas.

Also known as the eastern flower, lobster flower, Mexican frame leaf, and Christmas flower, poinsettias have been particularly popular in homes and churches. Its striking beauty, religious symbolism, and, of course, its Christmas colors have won it a special place in the hearts of everyone.

It is said that one Christmas long ago a little Mexican girl called Pepita was very sad. She desired, more than anything, to give a fine present to the Christ Child at the church service that evening. But she was very poor and had no gifts. As she walked sorrowfully to church with her cousin Pedro, he tried to console her.

"Pepita," he said, "I am certain that even the most humble gift, given in love will be acceptable in His eyes." So Pepita gathered a bouquet of common weeds from the roadside and entered the church.

As she approached the altar her spirits lifted. She forgot the humbleness of her gift as she placed it tenderly at the feet of the Christ Child.

Then there was a miracle! Pepita's insignificant weeds burst into brilliant bloom. They were called *flores de noche buena,* flowers of the holy night. We call them poinsettias.

The poinsettia (*Euphorbia pulcherrima*), is native to Mexico. When it was first cultivated by the Aztecs, it was called *Cuetlaxochiti* and was prized by them as a symbol of purity. They also recognized it for its practical value using the colorful bracts for dye and the milky latex in the stem for fever medicine.

It was not until the seventeenth century that Franciscan priests began to include poinsettias in their Christmas celebrations. They used them in the nativity procession in the Fiesta of Santa Pesebre.

Introduction of the poinsettias to the United States came by way of Joel Roberts Poinsett, who, when he died in 1851, was the last surviving member of a French Huguenot family which had settled in Charleston about 1697.

In his youth, Poinsett traveled extensively in Europe and Russia. He was sent, in 1811, as commercial agent for the United States to Argentina and Chile. In 1825, he was sent to Mexico as U.S. minister, returning in 1829. The preceding year he had sent back to Charleston a shipment of plants or seeds that was reputed to include cactuses, red and yellow mimosa, and "a species of hibiscus that changes from white to pink to red in a single day."

It was again discovered by Robert Buist of Philadelphia, who, within a few years, brought together a choice collection of plants. In turn, James McNab brought specimens of this collection to the Botanical Garden, Edinburgh, and to several other establishments in Scotland.

According to the botanical magazine of 1836, "this truly most magnificent of all tropical plants we have ever seen is crowned with flowers, surrounding which are bright scarlet whorls of bractae, frequently measuring 12 inches in diameter."

Another person instrumental in popularizing the plant in North America was Albert Ecke, who began flower farming in Hollywood in 1906. Already a fruit and vegetable grower, he started his flower fields with gladioluses, chrysanthemums, and poinsettias.

After he died in 1918, his dairyman son, Paul Ecke, decided to go into the flower business full-time. He chose to concentrate on the poinsettias and so developed a market for them.

When Paul Ecke was growing the poinsettia in California fields, they were being used for landscaping. He began to think there might be a market for producing the plants for commercial greenhouse growers in the Midwest and Eastern states. He was using the old varieties, which were pretty but did not hold their leaves well. They rarely held their foliage until Christmas, even in the greenhouse.

In 1923, Ecke obtained a new variety called oak leaf, the first of a series of improved varieties that held their foliage much better than the original plants. A whole new series of poinsettias were developed including, in 1963, the Paul Nicholson.

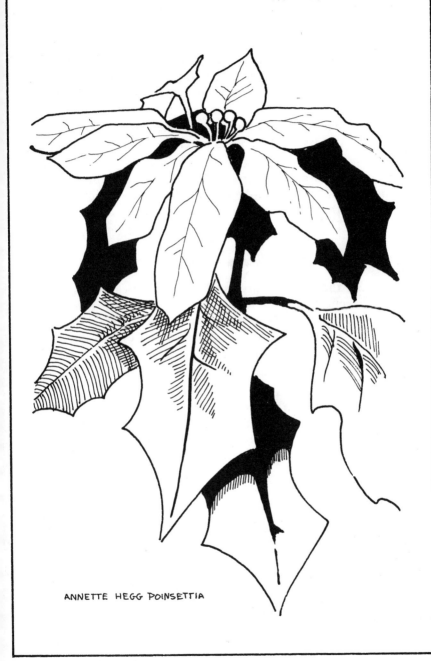

ANNETTE HEGG POINSETTIA

The most popular varieties now are the Annette Hegg group, of Norwegian origin. There are some Ecke poinsettias grown but the Annette Hegg is by far the most popular.

Annette Hegg red, Annette Hegg white, and Annette Hegg hot pink are just a few of the many types of poinsettias we have today. These improved varieties hold their colorful bracts for many months.

Development of new varieties takes at least 8 years. In the near future, consumers will be able to purchase the poinsettia in tree form.

It's quite natural that even serious gardeners take flowers and plants for granted, but someone, sometime, somewhere, worked long and hard to develop what we enjoy today.

Yuletide legends are always worth retelling

In 1933, the Junior Garden Club of America published an ancient legend about the Holy Trees of Christmas. I think the story is worth repeating now almost 50 years later, since every legend has its origin in some experience and belief founded in truth.

Since ancient days, people all over the world have enjoyed the cheerful greens of the pine, the fir, and the spruce.

When the wise men visited the Christ Child they brought with them gifts of gold and frankincense and myrrh—the most precious gifts they could think of for the Son of God. Have you ever wondered where one of these three wise men found this gift of frankincense?

On his way to Bethlehem, one of the wise men passed through a great pine forest and stopped before one of the trees, cutting a slit in the bark just long enought to allow the fragrant, yellow resin to ooze into a lovely old stone jar. The resin was called frankincense by the Hebrews.

Another beautiful old legend tells us that when Mary was fleeing with the Christ Child from the soldiers of the wicked King Herod, she came to a forest and was too weary to go on. And so with her baby she hid and rested in an open cavity of a great old pine. This ancient legend further says that the old tree, to prove the love of the plant world for human life, lowered its massive limbs concealing the precious family in its cool, fragrant arms until Herod's soldiers had passed.

In gratitude, the Christ Child raised his arms and blessed the old pine for its shelter and in doing so, marked the pine fruit with his hand. It is said that an imprint of the baby's hand can sometimes be found in the markings of the pine cone if you will cut it lengthwise.

As Christian history moved northward into Switzerland and Germany, we are told of thrilling Teutonic legends about the evergreens that clothed the famous Harz Mountains where our canaries come from.

A fierce winter storm was raging through these mountains. Each blast was filled with sleet and snow so heavy that massive trees were split and went crashing down the mountainsides. Only the fir trees with their deep, gnarled roots were able to withstand the cruel onslaught of the terrific gale. In each brief lull could be heard the distressing cry of the wind-tossed golden canaries. The great old fir trees heard it. As the wind blew through their needles, the firs' call was carried to the birds: "Come into my branches. We'll protect and care for you as our family has always cared for the earth's living things."

The poor little tired canaries, hearing the call, took their last bit of strength to fly into the protective arms of the trees to stay until the storm was over. "We will always make our homes with you, oh fir trees, and we will forever sing our praises to you as the sacred house of birds all over the world."

When your canary is singing his sweetest, you know he is singing about the fir trees that protected the Harz Mountains' canaries so many years ago.

Another delightful legend of the Harz Mountain firs tells of a poor miner's family. The father became ill, leaving his wife and children without food or fuel. Each morning the wife would climb one of these mountains to pick up some cones to sell as fuel for another day's living. As she entered the woods near Christmas day a little old imp named St. Nick jumped out from a fir tree and said to her: "Take only cones under this tree, for they are the best."

The woman thanked him, and as she started to pick up the cones there was such a downfall of them that she was frightened. Her basket was soon full. As she started home it became heavier and heavier until she could scarcely reach her door. When she emptied the cones on the table, every one of them was made of pure silver. Even now, fir cones are gathered and covered with a silver-like sulphur paint and sold in bags to burn and crackle in our Christmas fires.

St. Nick, the Harz Mountain imp, lived in the fir tree and became so famous that it has long been the custom of peasant girls to dance about the fir tree at their religious festivals, singing songs and decorating the tree with lights, flowers, eggs, and gewgaws. Thus they think that they hold good old St. Nick captive among its branches until he comes out and gives to them whatever is in his keeping before they will let him go free. This age-old custom is said to be the origin of the Christmas tree and the legend of old St. Nick.

Come Christmas, consider relating some of the delightful legends to your young children. I'm sure they'll be delighted, especially with the Harz Mountain canaries.

Hints on care of Christmas trees and plants

This is a good time to repeat a number of Christmas tips that will make the holidays safer and more pleasant.

Cut Christmas trees   Cut 1 inch (2.5 centimeters) off base of tree to freshly expose trunk. Use a stand with water holder or use a bucket with rocks to hold tree in place. Keep container filled with water. Tree preservatives especially for Christmas trees provide for further safety and lasting quality. Do not have flaming candles on the tree; use safe lights and check wiring and plugs for frays or other unsafe conditions.

It's hard to beat a blue spruce for a living Christmas tree.

Living Christmas trees A beautiful focal point in the home at Christmas and in the garden for years to come is a living tree. It is an investment in the landscape beauty and in the value of your home. Place tree in a water-tight container, such as a tub or pail, or a container with drainage that will take a good saucer. Soak root-ball thoroughly and keep moist throughout its stay indoors. Check ball daily; it may require 1 quart to 2 gallons (2 to 7.5 liters) of water every day, depending on the size of tree and container. As soon as possible after Christmas, move tree outdoors. Should the weather be very cold, move it gradually, first placing it in a garage, carport, porch, or other protected area for 10 to 12 days to acclimatize it. Keep root-ball moist, as before.

When planting outdoors, carefully remove tree from pot so as not to disturb soil from the roots. Do not remove any burlap from around the roots but do cut any twine that encircles the tree trunk. Plant so that the tree is no deeper in the garden soil than it was in the pot. Water the tree well and continue to water twice a week until established. Do not feed until spring.

Poinsettias   Poinsettias need moist air, so surround plant with sphaghnum moss if possible. Syringe leaves occasionally with tepid water (but not red leaves or flowers). Keep the area fairly warm and free of drafts. Water carefully, avoiding water-logging. Use tepid water and do not allow to dry out. You can keep your poinsettias for next year by keeping them in the house or setting them in the garden during summer. Bring them in in early fall and care for them then as per the instructions provided in the September section of Questions and Answers.

Hawaiian Christmas tree (Norfolk Island pine)   A popular indoor plant that has a lovely Christmas-tree shape and can easily be decorated for Christmas. Light should be indirect. Water with tepid water; rainwater is great. Water only when dry, but, during summer, water much more regularly. Use an acid fertilizer. Temperatures should be kept slightly cool.

Christmas cactus   This is a forest cactus. Choose a well-lit spot. Increase watering after resting period. Treat as an ordinary house plant. Water well when the soil begins to dry. February and March are rest months. Keep cool and water infrequently. In April and May, water thoroughly when compost begins to dry. From June to the middle of September, place in a shaded spot outside. From the middle of September to

246

the middle of November, keep dryish and cool until flower buds form, then increase watering and temperature. From the middle of November to February, treat normally.

Azalea   Countless azaleas are bought every year at Christmas time to bring decoration during the holiday season and into the New Year. Azaleas come in a variety of colors and combinations. Without correct care, you'll get flower and leaf drop. The secret in keeping a plant in bloom for many weeks and capable of coming back into flower the following year is to keep it wet (not just moist), cool, and brightly lit. Remove the old flowers.

Christmas peppers   This popular plant at Christmas provides much color. Peppers may bloom for many months. Give direct sunlight and keep the soil wet. Never allow to dry out. Hot, dry air will cause the fruit to fall.

Christmas cyclamen   Keep in fairly well-lit spot. cyclamen like a humid atmosphere and like it fairly cool. Water regularly from below using tepid water. Do not splash water on fleshy crown, as this could cause rot to set in and leaves to yellow and die. Remove dead flowers and feed during flowering season.

Citrus trees   There is an obvious fascination in having a lemon or orange tree in the home. A cultivated citrus will often take a number of years to bloom and bear fruit, which is why the variety calamondin is so popular.

The calamondin orange is more than ornamental; it blooms freely, bears lots, and has very fragrant blooms. The fruit, however, is bitter and small. Requirements are good drainage, careful watering, ample feeding, full sun, summers outdoors, and cool temperatures in winter.

Gardenia   The gardenia is a delight indoors. The

waxy white flowers surround the air with a delicate fragrance. The gardenia is somewhat temperamental, and therefore it is most important to follow the growing rules provided here from the experience of those who have learned the hard way.

For flowerbuds to form, a night-time temperature of 60-65°F (15-25°C) is required and the day temperature should be about 10°F (5°C) higher. An even temperature and careful watering are needed to prevent the buds from dropping off. Soft and tepid water must be used to prevent the foliage from turning yellow. The gardenia likes bright light, misting, and regular feeding with acid fertilizer.

A final word about bulbs

We've all heard it said that the best gifts come in small packages. This truly applies to bulbs.

Why in heaven did God hide such beautiful things as a tulip, daffodil, crocus, or gladiolus in such ugly shells? But, then again, we must remember another saying: beauty is more than skin deep. Some of the most beautiful people I have known are not the best looking physically. When we plant a Holland tulip bulb, it's just like burying a treasure.

Like any buried fortune, you must make a map so you don't forget where the bulbs are buried. When you go to plant your summer flowering bulbs, you should stake or mark them, preferably with the name so that a month later, when you go to plant the annuals, you'll not disturb the bulbs or plant the wrong annuals in front, thereby hiding the bulbous flowers when they begin to make a fabulous show.

So, if you haven't already marked where you've put your bulbs, do it now while you can still see where you've been working. With spring's growth you'll have a hard time recalling exact spots, or come spring, you'll find some overloaded areas and some with absolutely nothing.

Bulb blooming review

Here's how you can have a showing year round. Getting the right bulbs for the right month will assure beauty every month, and really, it's not all that much work.

In January, you can have a lovely show of winter crocus and snowdrops; even through the snow and frost their color and beauty will survive. In February, you can enjoy the winter aconites and chionodoxa, and perhaps the longest show of color comes from our rockery iris.

In March, the regular crocus, anemones, rockery daffodils, and tulips should be just super. In April enjoy all varieties and colors of daffodils and narcissuses both single and double, and hyacinths which will bring a fragrance beyond description.

In May, you can enjoy the tulips. In June, it's time for iris. July brings freesias, acidanthera, gladioluses, dahlias, and others. August will see a continuation of the July flowering bulbs and your show of dahlias is a blaze of color.

With the approach of our Indian summer, September will show more of the same: summer flowers plus a great show of alluim and, of special beauty, the fall crocus. In October and November, the bulb crop will be diminishing and then you'll be readying for spring; the final weeks of December again brings the first sign of color.

Now's the time to begin considering where to plant the summer and fall flowering bulbs. Planting time is April to May, but gladioluses, for example, can be planted at about 2 week intervals, thereby giving a continuous show of bloom starting in June through to October.

There you have it—a year of pleasurable chores that will insure year-round beauty in your yard and garden. Bedding plants, bulbs, hedges, evergreens, perennials, annuals—the list goes on and on. Because of dedicated horticulturists of the past and nurserymen of today, you have an inexhaustible supply of landscaping gems to brighten your environment.

I've know people who had never thought of growing things

until, just once, they tried some patio tomatoes. Then they tried a few other things, and from that time on they were addicted to gardening.

As I've said, not everyone will develop an active interest in growing things, but I've yet to see a person who will deliberately turn away from a bouquet or a little patch of colorful blooms. Somehow, flowers soften everyone's hearts. When you stop to think about it, there isn't an occasion, a holiday, a state or province, or a month, that isn't associated with a flower. There is no more universal symbol of beauty and affection on earth than the flower.

Q: I've decided to try a garden next spring, but I haven't very much space. What is the smallest plot to be practical?

A: Well, even window boxes will grow radishes and lettuce. A plot as small as 4 feet by 20 feet (1 meter by 6 meters) is practical, or even 10 feet (3 meters) if you grow the right things. Try pole beans and things that will train upwards on supports. Don't forget tomatoes, they don't take much room if staked and looked after. I'm sure a visit to a nursery, come spring, will reveal there are a lot of things that can be done with a very small plot. Maybe not practical for a big family, but certainly for two or three people; you'll find many small space items. One author of a garden book stated he had grown a thousand carrots in a 4 foot by 4 foot (1 meter by 1 meter) planter. That's a lot of carrots!

It's not so much the quantity, but the quality that counts. Experiment with all the goodies that go into crisp, fresh green salads, and I'm sure you'll find the tiniest garden is worth the effort.

Acknowledgments

A green thumb is contagious. And, once you've caught the disease, you will want everyone to catch it. Many never will, but I like to feel the opportunity given me by my community newspaper, *The Columbian*, may have spread enthusiasm for gardening. My thanks to the many readers who have written and expressed their joy in gardening, and to the listeners who have called with questions and comments during my guest appearances on Gary Bannerman's radio talk show.

My thanks also to the publisher, editor, and illustrator for their support and co-operation.

Bill Vander Zalm

Index

Strawberries   13-5-7
Grapes   2-14-6 or similar
Boysenberries   180 Q
Rose Food   186
Bulbs   191